Your Retail Store

An Owner's Manual

A–Z

by Robert Wells

with Illustrations by
Catherine (Cat) Meyer

Your Retail Store, an Owner's Manual A–Z

Published by RST Press
PO Box 272407
Houston TX, 77277-2407

Contents

Introduction

This manual is for all those brave entrepreneurs who have, or hope to have, a retail store of their own. It is designed to guide newcomers through unfamiliar waters, and to help experienced merchants to set the most profitable course.

Most books on starting and managing your own business seem more relevant to service industries and manufacturing than to retailing, and concentrate on fundamentals such as business plans, financing, and bookkeeping. These, tailored to your specific needs as a retailer, are fully discussed, but much attention is also paid to the "nitty-gritty" of everyday operations, such as how to deal with bounced checks, the keeping of a store diary, the comparative merits of tinted or clear glass windows, the need to provide chairs for customers, and many other details of the retailer's life which are not usually discussed in the "how to" books, but are nonetheless important.

Successful management is an art: all the colors on the manager's palette must be used to the full, and their properties understood, if a profitable picture is to be painted. The ones you will be using – Bookkeeping, Costing, Display, Housekeeping, Payroll, Personnel, Planning, Purchasing, Receiving, Selling, and the rest – are fully considered, with practical suggestions on how to apply them. You will become, if not fully expert in them all, certainly familiar with how they should be used, so that you can study further yourself, or delegate responsibilities, and be ready in any case to answer the most searching questions of an imaginary and demanding boss – for they are the sort of questions you must ask yourself every day.

You may feel that some topics are too elementary to deserve a place. They are included because I have myself ignored some of them to my cost (or at least annoying inconvenience), and have seen others suffer in the same way. It may seem ridiculous, for instance, to mention that you will need a telephone message pad, but business has been missed, and customers offended, because messages were written on scraps of paper which, of course, were lost. It may seem redundant, too, to emphasize the importance of computers, but again, I have known unfortunate business owners who scorned them. Lastly, nitpicking details on how to do daily chores such as Cashing Out are only suggestions based on what I have found quickest, easiest, and most accurate. You may have a better way, but there is no need to spend time reinventing the wheel.

The opinions expressed are based on twenty years experience in my retail store, and another twenty before that in retailing, manufacturing, and consulting. I had some successes, made many mistakes, and always profited from discussing both with friends and colleagues. I hope that you will add to that discussion, not only with your friends and associates, but also with me. Your criticism and comments will be appreciated.

There are as many reasons for opening your own retail store as there are different sorts of people, but there are two fundamental requirements: you must enjoy it, and you must make a profit. I hope that this manual will help you do both.

Robert Wells
Houston 1998

OPEN
Come On In!

A

ACCOUNTANT. It is up to you to make the money, but only your accountant (unless you are of that persuasion yourself) can ensure that every incoming and outgoing penny is recorded to the best possible advantage, considering tax law and your business structure (sole proprietor, partnership, corporation?), while at the same time providing you with the financial feedback so essential to success.

Bookkeeping (*which see*) is the simple recording of transactions. Accounting is arranging the records in the correct and most advantageous manner. For example, a retailer wants to enlarge his premises: the landlord agrees to do the work for $3,000, payable over twelve months. It is easy to record the transaction, but should it be entered as an Expense, or as a Leasehold Improvement? The recording is bookkeeping. Answering the question is Accounting.

In choosing an Accountant it is tempting to go first-class, and retain a big, well-known firm, but the fame and profits of such firms do not come from serving small retailers. Your little account, after a charming introductory meeting with one of the principals, will probably be handled by a junior who will not (and should not) remain junior for long, and you will find yourself talking to a different person every time you call.

Find a CPA who will handle your account personally, stay with you, get to know you, ask questions and take an interest in your business, pointing out problems and opportunities which you might otherwise have missed.

Your Accountant can make a much more positive contribution to the success of your business than merely preparing Tax Returns.

ACCOUNTS. These are described under Financial Statement. If you feel that they involve mere bean-counting, better left to your CPA, remember that you need as much information about your business as a doctor needs about his patient: timely Accounts give you the information you need for the health and body-building programs which will make your business grow.

Your Accounts, although prepared in the shape required by law, are yours, for your use: your Tax Returns, and the Accounts from which they are drawn, are far more useful to you than to the government. It pays to study them, and to understand (in discussion with that excellent Accountant) their implications.

Business management is much more than mere bean-counting, but to manage well you do have to know how to count the beans.

ACCOUNTS PAYABLE: You will see this term in all bookkeeping text books and computer programs It refers only to bills that are payable monthly, which will nearly all be vendors' accounts for merchandise, but will also include the light bill, telephone, etc.

ADVERTISING. Doing business without advertising, it has been said, is like winking at a girl in the dark: you know what you are doing, but nobody else does.

So you will have to advertise, and books on retailing will suggest a certain percentage of Gross Sales for this as for other Expenses, but before even considering any actual expenditure, your need to identify you store's position in the marketplace, and the image you want to project into that marketplace.

"Positioning yourself in the marketplace" sounds like Madison Avenue jargon, but all it means is that you cannot please all the people all the time. You have to decide either what sort of store you want, and then identify its market, or you must select a market, and then create a store to suit it.

Either way, your inventory, your decor, your location and your management style will combine to form a unique image, and your advertising must do two things: it must project that image, and it must project it to the right target – the chosen market.

Consistency in projecting the Image is critically important. Every printed advertisement must be instantly recognizable and invite closer reading; all radio commercials must be in a recognizable style, and compel the listener's attention.

The actual content of the advertisement, in whatever medium, will depend upon what you are trying to achieve. Do you want to concentrate on creating the Image, or sell large quantities of a particular item, or tell people for the first time of the existence of your store, or simply announce a Sale, or a Special Event? Every advertisement must have one overriding purpose, and that may well influence the choice of medium.

The choice is broad: there are Television, Radio, Periodicals, Newspapers, Billboards, Direct Mail, the Yellow Pages, Mobile Curbside Signs, Captive Balloons, Searchlights and Sky-Writing, with all their possible permutations and combinations (but I will let you do your own research on the last three).

Television, for a single owner-operated retail store, is probably too expensive, but its impact is undeniably the strongest of all the media. If you can afford a short campaign, it may be just what is needed to give a new business a catapult launch, or an existing one an extra boost. While the cost of air time depends on the market, production costs, with equipment constantly becoming smaller, lighter, and more easily portable, may be less daunting than they used to be, so it is worth investigating television before assuming that you cannot afford it. Also, in-house production by the station itself will save you money compared to a commercial studio, although the latter can produce more elaborate results if you are prepared to pay for them.

Radio has one cardinal virtue: it is the one medium in which your ad can cost you just what is on the rate card – nothing more – no production costs. It also, in my experience, produces more response than any print advertising except direct mail, and is the most flexible medium of all. You can change the copy at short notice with no more trouble than writing and, if you like, reading it. You will, of course, run into production costs if you want to be elaborate, with special music and a professional reader, but that is your choice.

Before selecting a radio station, explore the wavebands. Most of us tend to stay tuned to just one station, and there is a lot going on out there that we miss. It pays to listen around for a while to find out who is advertising what to whom in which radio format. You may find that your own favorite radio station is not necessarily the one best suited to your intended clientele. When you have reached a decision, however, a call to the station will get an account executive to your office on the double, with a media kit containing a full demographic analysis of the station's listeners, plus a rate card (the more spots per month, the lower the rate), and all other details, such as seasonal promotions, and special deals connected to current public events. You may also find that the account executive is prepared to work with you on an individual package deal, and give you rates more favorable than those shown on the rate card.

As in all advertising, and perhaps in radio more than most, persistence pays. To get results, you need to broadcast for at least a month, and preferably year round. This does not necessarily mean vast expense, for frequency is not as important as just keeping going. When I was on an annual contract of only two or three spots a week many customers remarked that they heard my ads "all the time."

This response even increased after the two spots were both broadcast on one day each week, rather than singly on separate days. There is no doubt that "grouping" in this way creates the maximum possible impact for low frequency programs, and even at higher frequencies it is more effective to bunch all spots in two or three days, rather than spread them over the week.

Rates vary for broadcasting at different times of day, being most expensive, of course, during prime time, but if you do want to pay more for a particularly favorable time, you may get mostly the same listeners every day, whereas if you let the station air the spots at random (omitting the middle of the night) you may spread the word more widely at less expense. The decision will depend upon how precisely you are able to identify your target audience and its listening habits.

Periodicals: the one word is quite inadequate to cover the multitude of advertising opportunities which it represents. There are national, state and local "glossies" for every imaginable taste and audience, and in them you will find every size and description of advertisement from full page full color to 3-line classified. If you are not already a magazine reader get a pile of them – even ones you think are quite irrelevant – and go through the ads: you may be surprised, and find some quite unexpected selling ground, and in any case you will almost certainly get ideas on layout and design.

Again, persistence pays, and rates drop for quantity. Twelve insertions in a monthly will be at a much better rate than just one or two. Remember, though, that the monthly rate is only half the story: this is where you pay production costs – not much, perhaps, for a little black and white, but substantial if there is much art work, and very substantial if you want color.

Billboards cannot, I believe, provide effective advertising within the normal budget of a small independent retailer unless, perhaps, there is particularly difficult problem with location, when a billboard, strategically placed, may guide customers to the door.

Direct Mail is always (after Television), the most effective way of getting your message to existing and potential customers. Production and postage, however, are not cheap, and if you are just starting out it may not be easy to identify your intended clientele, or to find the mailing list to match it, which in itself may be costly. It is a different matter if you have been in business for a while, because you will (won't you?) have built your own list by putting address cards on the counter for customers to fill out, and by photocopying all checks (which can also do away with tedious hand-listing for the Bank Deposit).

A computer and printer (*which see*) capable of desktop publishing will enable you to design and produce your own mailing pieces, catalogs, etc., and print the mailing labels, but to justify the purchase three conditions must be met:

- You (or one of your staff) must have the skill and aptitude to make full use of them.

- Your planned mailings must be sufficiently frequent to keep them economically busy.

- The cost must be within your Budget.

You may plan to send out regular mailings, or occasional ones for Special Events, or irregular ones geared to the year's Sales Peaks (*which see*), or any combination of these, but whatever the immediate purpose of the mailing it must achieve at least one of three purposes: first, of course, it should persuade the recipient to do what it asks; failing that, it should at least persuade her to read it, and failing that, at the very least, it should leave a lasting impression of your Business Name on her memory.

If it is in an envelope it may well fail on all counts, unless your mailing list is small enough to enable you to use first-class stamps, and to write the addresses by hand, when it will not look like junk mail. A "self-mailer," with the address on the piece itself, will save the cost of envelopes and of stuffing them, and will at least be seen as it is taken from the mail box. If it is sufficiently attractive, colorful and well designed it will leave some sort of impression even if it is just glanced at and thrown away. Its chances of being read will greatly improve if you adopt a distinctive style for all mailings, with consistently recognizable and attractive design, so that eventually recipients will ask "Who *are* these guys?," and do something about finding out.

The Yellow Pages are certainly effective for the customer looking for professional help – doctors, lawyers, accountants – or for service industries such as plumbers, cleaners and auto repair. In a resort area with heavy tourist traffic they may also be very helpful to the visitor looking for conventional retail and gift shops. The value for you of advertising in The Yellow Pages will depend very much on the character of your community.

Mobile Curbside Signs do not project the sort of image normally connected with more affluent communities and their up-market shopping centers: indeed it is not unusual to see a clause in the leases for such centers, specifically banning their use.

One delightful, if dangerous, aspect of selecting advertising media is that all the sales people concerned are passionately and sincerely convinced that their own medium is the best and most effective, and the one most perfectly suited to your particular needs. The trouble is, some of them may be right. Your mission, should you choose to accept it, is to decide which.

ADVERTISING AGENTS AND DESIGN STUDIOS. Do not neglect the services of these experts; they know a lot more about advertising than you do. On the other hand, you know a lot more about your business than they do. If you decide to use them, make sure that you select one which will listen to you as much as advise you. A good Agent will not only handle the content and design of advertisements for all media, but will also know which medium will be most effective for a particular purpose. He will help, too, in long-term planning, to ensure that the year's Advertising Budget is spent to best advantage. The decision on whether to use an Agent or Studio, as indeed all decisions on advertising, will depend on the size of your Budget, and on a shrewd assessment of costs and benefits, but however shrewd your financial analysis, advertising remains in some ways rather like religion: you either have Faith, or you don't, and in any case it is difficult to measure results.

To find the best Agency, study the advertising in your area, and pick out the advertisements which most excite you. Even if it turns out that the agency concerned is too expensive for you, it should always be possible to buy or beg an hour of their time, and ask what they would do in your place, and on your budget. After all, if their advice is good, you should be coming back to them as a customer in a year or two.

ANNIVERSARIES. Make the most of your Anniversaries. Have some Special Event on the anniversary of your Opening Day, and give all the ladies a nice red rose and all the children a balloon (it is surprisingly inexpensive to have balloons printed with your Name and Logo, and to rent a helium cylinder for the day). If you can think of something more imaginative than roses and balloons, and of anything at all for the men, you will be doing better than most.

For any special milestone in the history of your store, plan a celebration and issue a Press Release to get the media interested. Your local paper particularly, will probably be glad to feature your store as a new member of the community, or salute it as an old friend.

The history of your State will probably yield some popular historical Anniversaries, and if you or your customers have any particular relationship with foreign countries, you can celebrate their national Anniversaries, such as Bastille Day for France or the Queen's Birthday for Britain.

A display of flags always attracts attention, and you can get all shapes sizes and nationalities, from little paper flags on toothpicks to full-sized real ones. A very popular table decoration is the 4×6 flag on a miniature flag-pole. A quantity of them all round the store creates a very cheerful impression, and is also a wonderfully effective way of advertising that there's something special going on. *See also* Events.

An Anniversary is a ready-made marketing opportunity. Take full advantage of it by selecting merchandise and an advertising theme relevant to the occasion, and make a profit out of a celebration which both you and your customers will enjoy. (*See also Sales Peaks*)

ANNUAL COMPARISONS: The true measure of performance is comparison with the previous year. All Financial Statements have two columns, one for the current year, and one for the previous year, giving full details of Sales, expenses and all other factors. The importance of some of these is discussed under Balance Sheet in Financial Statements, and others are mentioned under Diary which shows non-financial comparisons day by day, such as a flood last year to explain the great increase in Sales this year. Two extremely useful comparisons which do not appear in the Financial Statement are Sales per Square Foot, and Sales per Hour, which can be shown monthly. The advantage of Sales per Square Foot is that it shows increase or decrease regardless of the size of the store, so that if that has changed, the comparison remains valid. The advantage of Sales per Hour is that it shows true sales performance regardless of the length of the month or changes in business hours. It does not take long, at the beginning of the year, to calculate Business Hours per month, taking holidays etc., into account. (*See* Appendix, p. 200.)

Not many retailers, for instance, have accurate knowledge of monthly sales variations. December, for most, will be the busiest, and one can usually have a fairly good feel for other seasonal variations, but how many retailers can rate all the months on a scale of one to twelve? A simple graph will show the year's activity, and if it is based on Sales per Hour it will be entirely accurate, regardless of the number of days in the month or other differences which invalidate comparisons of mere monthly sales figures. *See* Sales per Square Foot *and* Sales per Hour.

ANSWERING MACHINE. When I was running my own store I would often get to work early, to have quiet time for office work, or to change displays, before opening at nine. Nearly always customers would call, expressing no surprise at getting an answer (although they would have been astonished to find the front door open at that hour) and the same would happen if I stayed late. Obviously many calls out of business hours were going unanswered, and the case for an Answering Machine became unanswerable.

The Answering Machine is misnamed. For our purposes it should be called the Information Machine, the Public Relations Machine, or the Marketing Machine. A friendly, informative message will, for instance, bring the caller to the store if it is open on one of those holidays when many stores are closed; or it may bring her in if she thought you opened at ten, like your neighbors, but learns from the Machine that you actually open at nine. With the basic information (which, of course, you must keep up-to-date) you can include a short – it must be short – advertisement for an upcoming Event, or a new line of merchandise, or a Sale.

The Answering Machine will more than earn its keep by contributing to Public Relations and Advertising. Don't waste it by simply having it recite your business hours.

ANTICIPATION: You will sometimes see, on an invoice, some such words as "Terms: Net 30. No Anticipation." This means that you cannot unilaterally take a percentage discount if you pay sooner. For that to be possible, the Invoice must say "2/10, Net 30," or similar, when you can deduct 2% if you pay within ten days of the Invoice date.

ASSETS. You have important Assets other than those listed by your Accountant (for those, *please see* Balance Sheet), and they should be recognized and nurtured so that they make the fullest possible contribution to the business. They are listed under this slightly unconventional heading to emphasize their value.

Your greatest and most important non-financial Asset should be your own personality. If it is not, you are almost certainly in the wrong business. There is no specific type of personality ideally suited to retailing, but there is one basic requirement: you must love retailing.

You must enjoy the company of your customers, your staff, and your suppliers; you must take an interest in the nature of your merchandise, and appreciate its quality and value; you must be sensitive to the requirements of display, Layout and Lighting, and you have to revel in the delights of accurate records and bookkeeping and their perusal, for they are the instruments which monitor the health of your business, and which provide the information essential to successful planning.

You must, in short, combine the talents of the businessman, the psychologist, and the artist, and with it all maintain a genial disposition. If indeed you possess all these talents, you are an impossible paragon, but if you understand their importance and their desirability, you can assemble the right people around you, and build your second greatest Asset – your Staff.

If you and your staff enjoy coming to work, if your customers enjoy shopping at your store, and if sales representatives look forward to calling on you, then you are making the most of your Assets.

ASSORTMENTS. Some merchandise, coffee mugs for instance, may only be available in assortments, packed six to a box, with two each of three different patterns. Be cautious in your buying if this is the case, as you may well find that two of the three patterns sell very well, while the third stays on the shelf, and you cannot reorder the good ones without getting more of the duds. It is always worth asking the vendor to supply the good patterns in boxes of six to a pattern, but if this does not work you simply have to stop carrying what could have been a profitable item. If this happens, it is worthwhile writing to the vendor to explain why you have stopped ordering the assortment.

Another type of Assortment which presents problems is the seasonal special deal. This typically will consist of a whole range of merchandise – six of this, twelve of that, nine of the other, and so on, with some free items added, or a special price for the whole deal. Again, this Assortment may contain nine excellent items, and one dud. Unlike the coffee mugs, which inexplicably continue to be made, the duds in this assortment may well be discontinued items which the vendor is trying to get rid of: if you get them free this does not matter – you can gain PR points by giving them away, or perhaps put a price on them and reap some extra profit. If, however, the deal rests solely on a special price, analyze its composition very carefully. There is no point in buying it at the special price if it merely compensates you for getting unsaleable items.

There can be a costly delay in pricing this type of assortment because the sales representative will probably have written the order as "Assortment CH23, $500," without itemizing the contents. When the goods arrive, the Packing List and Invoice will be no more informative, and you will have to find the original brochure (if the representative left it with you) before you can check quantities and prices of individual items, so make sure, when the representative writes the order, that it is itemized, showing individual prices.

This is not a trivial point: such an order would probably be for seasonal merchandise, and be placed at a busy time of year, and the last thing you want at such a time is a $1,000 assortment stuck in an overcrowded stock room for want of prices, when it should be out on the shop floor earning a profit.

This emphasizes one of the most important axioms of retailing:

Merchandise in the stockroom does not earn its keep

Car makers realized years ago the road to profit was "just in time" inventory control, where parts are delivered straight to the production line in the quantities immediately needed, with none in reserve. The same applies to retailing: purchasing must be scheduled so that all merchandise goes straight into the showroom, with none left in the stockroom. Of course there will have to be exceptions, but they must be made only in the clear knowledge that they are exceptions, and that the rule is being broken.

AUTHORIZATION. If you accept credit cards and use a hand imprinter you will probably be required by the Card company to telephone for authorization of any sale over the amount of your "Floor Limit," perhaps $50 or $75, depending on the volume of business with that card. If you fail to do so the card company can refuse to honor the sale.

This tedious process is virtually obsolete, as most card sales are now entered electronically, which includes automatic authorization. *See* Credit Cards.

Barcode

B

BACK ORDERS. You will not always get everything you order: missing items may be actually missing (shown as shipped on the Packing List, and charged on the Invoice, but not received – *see* Claims), but usually you will find either a note on the documents saying "Items not shipped are out of stock. Please re-order," or you will find that the missing items are shown as "Back-ordered," which means that they will be shipped automatically when available, unless you specified "No Back Orders" on your Purchase Order.

If you do opt for "No Back Orders" on one Purchase Order, you may well find that your whole file with that vendor has been so marked. Not only will there be nothing back-ordered in future, but all earlier back-orders outstanding will be canceled, which may be embarrassing if customers are waiting for them.

The back-order system can be very convenient, but on a big order small batches or even single items can keep coming for months, and unless you have been keeping very strict records, you may think yourself out of stock and re-order, only to have an old back-order come in the next day. This not only ties up more money in Inventory than you intended, but also damages Cash Flow, as the back-order presents you with a bill you were not prepared for.

Another drawback of back orders is that the small follow-up shipments will often bear their own separate freight charges, which can seriously diminish Profit. It has even been known for vendors to apply a "small order surcharge" to back-order shipments, from an original order which was well over the minimum. This is probably caused by computer error rather than deliberate villainy, but is nonetheless infuriating and costly, both in itself and in the correspondence to rectify it. It is also a charge which may slip through unnoticed if you do not keep a very sharp eye on your Invoices.

As back-order service is much better from some vendors than others, it pays to decide on its use vendor by vendor, rather than lay down a general policy.

BACK-UP: Back up your computer files daily, or at least weekly, and keep copies of the disks or tapes off premises. Copies in the store should be in a fire resistant file or cabinet.

BAD CHECKS. You will get some. If you are lucky you will have a clientele which only bounces checks by mistake, and you will get an apologetic telephone call before a check comes back from the bank. Sometimes, though, you will have to be firm. Be polite to start with: you can always get tough later. Start out tough, and you can lose a good customer who has made an honest mistake – or whose bank has made a mistake. First, for instance, ask the bank whether the check can be redeposited, because customers will sometimes ask you to send it through again, and you need to be able to tell them that it is truly unacceptable. Also, the bank will charge you (as well as the customer) a fee for a bad check, and you need to make it clear to the customer at once that you expect her to pay that. If she is really difficult, you may have to send the check to the bank "for collection." There is a fee, but you will get most of the money you are owed, and the customer is made aware that checks are not bounceable at your store.

If the amount is large, you may decide to file suit, perhaps in Small Claims Court. The details of the procedure, such as the minimum amount of the sale, and whether you have to show proof of what actual items were bought, may vary from state to state. Ask your attorney for details, but don't wait until you have a problem: make sure that you know all your options to start with. This will save time, and will give you the upper hand when discussing repayment with the customer.

Occasionally the account has closed, and the criminal gone. All you can do is write off the loss.

You can avoid all this by subscribing to a credit service: all checks are authorized at time of sale, and the credit service accepts the risk. First, though, add up your actual bad check losses over a period (including Christmas, the high season for check-bouncing), and make sure that they are greater than the credit service fee.

For a new business, the decision on use of a credit service is not so easy, but discussions with neighboring merchants would probably be helpful, and the decision is in any case reversible.

BAD DEBTS: Any money which you are owed and which you cannot collect is, of course, a bad debt, and will be recorded as such by your accountant. If you carry charge accounts, for instance, one or two will become delinquent, and be classified as bad debts; but be alert for the less obvious ways in which you can lose money. You may be short-shipped, and the expected credit, refund or replacement may not come; or your advertisement may be printed wrong, or your custom-printed bags may not be to specification, or your damage claim to the trucking company may be neglected, or your insurance claim delayed, or any one of a hundred other possible proofs of Murphy's Law may have occurred. In every single instance you will be owed cash or credit or goods, and if you cannot collect you will have in effect, if not in name, a bad debt on your hands. Keep an eagle eye on all this potential leakage. The price of profit is eternal vigilance.

BAGS: You will put your customers' purchases in free bags which cost you money, but the extra cost if you put your logo on them will be repaid by the advertisement as they are carried down the street, and by the reminder to the customer at home.

You have a choice of paper or plastic, two-color or four-color, printed one or both sides, and of a variety of shapes, sizes, strengths, and handle designs. Your decision will be a compromise between what you want and what your budget allows, balancing three factors: the design and quality of the bag itself; the cost and quantity of the vendor's minimum order requirement; and how long the quantity will last. Your choice of paper and/or plastic (do not forget environmental reasons, or the desire to give your customers a choice) may also be affected by the fact that plastic takes up only a fraction of the storage space needed for paper.

You may also, of course, sell deluxe custom totes bearing your name and logo, and these can be in canvas or heavy cloth as well as paper or plastic. Beware though of embarking on this quite costly project too soon. The only reason that customers buy that sort of tote, unless it is of quite exceptionally attractive design, is to boast that they have shopped at your store, so you will not sell many before you have established a reputation for them to boast about.

You can certainly carry vendors' stock designs of deluxe totes, and generate substantial sales by selling them on their own, or as quick and easy substitutes for Gift Wrap. There are many extremely attractive designs on the market in sizes from miniature to huge, and they are more profitable and less labor-intensive than giftwrap.

You may also wish to offer these totes pre-packed as attractive ready-made gifts, and these can be particularly effective if sealed with your store label.

Both as substitute for giftwrap, and for pre-packed gifts, deluxe totes are extremely useful in saving both your time and the customer's, and they will gain you much business by establishing your reputation as a good place to find a nice gift in a hurry.

BANK: The same considerations apply to choosing a bank as to choosing an accountant. In both cases you need not an institution, but a person who will get to know you and your business over a period of years. "Small Business" to a big bank is usually something much bigger than a single retail store: you are more likely to find an understanding and enduring ear in a small independent bank, if there are any left. Simple convenience, however, will play a part in your selection: you will need to make a deposit every day, probably on the way home, and what may seem like a small detour to the bank of your choice when you are planning can become a major nuisance when you do it for the hundredth time after a hard day's work. You can, however, use a convenient bank for daily deposits, and make regular bulk transfers to your main bank.

This will, of course, apply only to deposits of cash and checks. Electronic Credit Card deposits can go straight to the Main bank.

BALANCE SHEET: *see* Financial Statement.

BANK DEPOSITS. In every sport there are some basic rules which the coach will drum into you day after day. In retailing there are two: reconcile the register, and *make the bank deposit.* It helps to have a spare cash drawer, so that you can close out the register and count the full drawer ahead of time, and have the bank deposit complete by the end of the day, ready for the night drop on the way home. You may prefer to make the deposit during the day, if the bank is conveniently close, rather than stopping at a lonely night-deposit box after dark. *Please see* Reconciling the Register.

BAR CODES. If you have computerized Inventory Control, it is virtually essential to have a Bar Code Reader, otherwise the cashier will have to key in the SKU number for every item. There are, however, no hard-

and-fast rules about this. I know one family-owned business with two large stores and at least eight cashiers in each, and the SKU number of every item is keyed in, from $2 hardware to $1,000 gifts. There is not a bar code reader to be seen. Use of bar codes is discussed more fully under computers, *which see.*

BASKETS. Even in a small store shopping baskets can increase sales. Customers appreciate having them, and will not be tempted to dump an armful of merchandise at the register and block the next sale, while they continue shopping. Also they will buy more altogether, and will come back because they find shopping at your store easy and comfortable. Try to find attractive wicker baskets rather than the standard plastic type: they are lighter to carry, they last for a very long time, and they add a touch of character. Also, if they suit your store, you may sell them, and their use for shopping will advertise them wonderfully.

BIMONTHLY. Twice a month. *See* Payroll.

BOOKKEEPING. Bookkeeping, the recording of financial transactions, is the arrangement of those transactions in the manner most advantageous to you, within the limits of tax law, in preparation for Accounting. There is no hard and fast division between Bookkeeping and Accounting: at one extreme you may simply hand to your CPA the month's sales records, invoices, check book and bank statement, in which case he will do both Bookkeeping and Accounting, and at the other you may do everything yourself, including tax returns, on a computer program such as Quickbooks™ or Peachtree™. Usually the basic bookkeeping will be done in house, and the results processed into Tax Returns and Financial Statements by the CPA.

In-house bookkeeping is much easier, quicker, and more useful to management than it used to be now that we have computers, and the good programs certainly live up to their claims of being easy to use, but they will not tell you, for instance, into which account you should put monthly payments for a new air conditioner – Capital or Expense – or whether the interest only should be Expensed, and the principal be put in Capital; and this itself may depend upon whether the agreement was lease-purchase, or straight monthly pay-out. The allowable depreciation rate, too, will have to be checked. However good the computer program, it will not answer all such questions, and you will need the help of a CPA. *See*

Accountant, Accounts, Chart of Accounts, Financial Statement.

There are always stories of eccentric millionaires who do all their bookkeeping with a pencil stub on the back of an envelope, but that will not do for the small retailer, who must keep proper records if he hopes to become a millionaire himself.

BOUNCED CHECKS. *See* Bad Checks.

BREAK EVEN POINT. The Break Even Point – the point at which Income equals Expenditure – is the single most critical factor in deciding whether a business, either projected or in being, can succeed, because it tells you the amount of Gross Sales needed to pay the bills. Planning a new business, or judging an existing one, is obviously impossible if you don't know this vital figure.

It is also invaluable as a measure of performance in a going concern, because lowering the Break Even Point means that fewer sales are needed to break even, so there is greater potential for profit. If you were manager of a branch and could show head office a continuing reduction in your break even point, you would get a medal.

Only two figures are needed to establish the Break Even Point: the amounts of the Overhead, and of the Gross Profit (or Gross Margin, if expressed as a percentage). Overhead will be a known dollar amount, reasonably reliable in a plan, and quite exact for an existing business. Gross Profit – what is left from Sales after paying for the goods sold – will be projected as a percentage in a plan but, like Overhead, should be accurately known in an existing business.

As Breaking Even simply means that <u>Gross Profit must equal Overhead</u>, the calculation is simple:

Example

To Break Even if Overheads are \$325,000 and projected Gross Margin is 45%, Sales must be \$722,222.22.

Sales: what Gross Profit [= Overhead] is 45% of:	722,222.22
Less Cost of Goods Sold: Sales less Gross Profit	– 397,222.22
Gross Profit: projected 45% of Sales,	325,000.00
Less Overhead: **the only known dollar amount**	– 325,000.00
Net Income (Profit or Loss)	0.00

Having established the Gross Sales needed to break even, you must now decide whether it is possible to do better, and make a profit. If, for instance, your type of store in your location can normally be expected to gross $240 per sq. ft. per year, and your Break Even Gross Sales come out at $500 per sq. ft., you are in trouble. (Sales per Sq. ft. = Gross Sales divided by total rented square footage: *e.g.* if you are paying rent for 2,500 sq. ft., and Sales are $600,000, Sales per sq. ft. = $240 per year).

The purpose of the break even point is to establish profit potential.

Profit can be achieved in only three ways:
Increasing Sales
Increasing Gross Margin
Decreasing Overhead

All these should be pursued simultaneously and constantly, but any one of them will increase profit if the other two do not change. Increased Sales, for instance, will not help if gross margin goes down. *See also* Growth.

Do not omit Depreciation (*which see*) from this break even calculation. Even though it is not a cash expenditure, it must be taken into account in your planning. The only time to omit Depreciation is in the Cash Flow Forecast.

BRIDAL REGISTRY. Do not assume that yours is not the type of store for a bridal registry. Nowadays it is increasingly common, even fashionable, for brides to register at all sorts of stores, for everything from linens to kitchenware – and if I had a hardware store I would open a registry for bridegrooms. Customers need not register just for *wedding gifts*: you can run a general *gift registry* also, where the scope is even greater.

For a Bridal Register, apart from details of the merchandise, you will need at least the date of the wedding, the bridegroom's name, the address to which gifts should be sent, and the bride's telephone number.

The bride will supply her list of wants, and careful record must be kept of what has been bought by whom, so that donors can be told what is still needed.

For wedding gifts that have to be specially ordered, and cannot arrive in time, you should have an expensively printed or engraved card, to be displayed among the gifts at the reception, showing what has been given by whom, and, of course, the name of your store.

BRIDGING LOAN. *See* Loans.

BROKER. You will probably do much buying in the nearest Trade Center, such as Dallas, Atlanta, Chicago, New York or Los Angeles. Some showrooms will belong to large manufacturers such as Waterford or Fitz & Floyd, displaying their own wares, but most will be under the names of Brokers, who will display and take orders for a broad range of goods from many different manufacturers or importers.

The showroom, whether manufacturer's or Broker's, has no inventory: it is there solely to display samples (the broker's eternal cry is that samples of the new patterns are late for the show), take orders, and be your personal contact with the vendor's head office and warehouse, which will probably be inconveniently remote.

Showrooms vary enormously in size. Some are operated by the owner-broker himself, who will be out on the road between shows, calling on you and his other customers, while others employ large traveling sales forces. There are, surprisingly, some brokers who neither travel themselves nor employ sales people. You will never know they or their products exist unless you search them out in the Trade Center itself. They will, however, be paid a commission on every sale in their territory, regardless of whether they themselves took the order. On the other hand a good broker or company sales person can be an enormous help, knowing more about his territory and your business than remote head office ever could, and acting as an invaluable mediator and go-between if there is a problem (living up to his name, in a slightly different sense, as an "honest broker").

Remember that although you have no financial relationship with the Broker, he will probably write your order on his own printed form bearing his own name, writing in by hand the name of the actual vendor. It pays to re-write that name large and bold on your copy, so that it gets filed accordingly, and is easily found when the goods arrive.

BUDGET. The trouble with budgets is that expenses can be forecast quite accurately, but future sales can only be a guess, particularly when you are just starting. That is not to say that you should not make budgets, and set sales targets, but they must be constantly updated in light of experience.

There are two ways to set up a budget. One is to use the budget facility in whatever bookkeeping software you may be using. This will give excellent results if the program accommodates all your needs, but the structure is usually fairly rigid, and not easily adaptable, if at all, to specialized requirements. In particular, it will probably be inextricably linked to data from existing operations, and it will not be possible to use it for unlimited "what-if" budgets based simply on projections.

For the purely projected Budget, which will give data and comparisons not available from the bookkeeping program, a spreadsheet such as Microsoft Excel™ or Lotus 1-2-3™ is needed. You can lay out all operational expenses and projected sales, play "what-if" with variations on all the figures, and watch the instantaneous change in the bottom line every time you alter a single figure. Like an aircraft simulator, you can fly your business through every conceivable permutation and combination of sales figures, fluctuating expenses, and changing tax codes before you settle on the structure which is most achievable.

All that effort will be wasted, however, if the Spreadsheet Budget is not set up in exactly the same basic format as the reports from the bookkeeping program.

The following is a sample spreadsheet.

Budget/Actual performance 1998

	January			February ...			Year-to-Date		
	Budget	Actual	% ±	Budget	Actual	% ±	Budget	Actual	% ±
Gross Sales									
Cost of Goods Sold									
Gross Profit									
Expenses (*Itemized...*)									
Net Income									

January, of course, will not need the YTD columns, but you will need six columns for the remaining months, making 69 columns in all. The tedious part is setting up the formulas in the spreadsheet so that the effect of every single entry carries through automatically to its own column totals, and to the percentage change and YTD columns. This, however, only has to be done once.

Setting up your Budget in this way, with instant comparison between aim and performance, ensures the tightest possible control. It is no good preparing a Budget which cannot be compared directly with the performance shown in the bookkeeping program's Income Statement (Profit and Loss Account).

BUSINESS PLAN. It is not worth even starting to think about raising capital without a Business Plan, and even if you are financing the enterprise yourself, you will need one so that you can set up a Budget.

Your public library will have several books on how to compile the most effective Business Plan, so I will mention here only the basic framework, which will, of course, vary depending on the nature of the business. Start with...

- **The Concept** – explain the goal – what sort of business is this going to be? This should be a brief introductory description of the whole enterprise. Next,

- **The Objective** – within so many years to have achieved such-and-such. Then,

- **The Timetable** – specify the nature and timing of steps planned to achieve the objective.

- **The Customers** – who you are aiming at; incomes, age-groups, trendy, conservative, arty, sporty, feminine, masculine, sophisticated, country. Your concept is wonderful: what sort of people will it appeal to? Where will you find them?

- **Location** – this ties in closely with Customers – describe the neighborhood, residential and commercial; quote any demographics you can find from the Chamber of Commerce or local Realtors. If you intend to lease in a mall or a shopping center, the owners will provide you with extensive information. Remember the three keys to success in retailing: location, location and location. Analyze potential competitors in the area; talk to neighboring merchants.

- **The Inventory** – describe in broad terms the type of inventory you intend to carry, pointing out the reasons with reference to customers and location.

- **The Marketing Advantages** – list the advantages your store will have as a result of your particular concept, supported by your research into the type of customer you hope to attract, in the location you have chosen, with the type of inventory you have selected. Will it be notably superior to any perceived competition, will it break new ground and be successful because it is something new and exciting in retailing, or will it simply be the only store of its type in the area?

You now need to enlarge on that broad summary, by including detailed sections on Inventory; Merchandise sources; Lay-out and appearance of premises and equipment; Administration and Staff; Management Philosophy; Advertising and Marketing Strategy; the business structure (proprietorship, partnership, corporation?), and any other aspect of the business which you feel needs to be described in more detail.

Having described what you want to do, how and when you want to do it, the timetable to achieve it, the reasons it will be successful, and the details of its inventory, design, staffing and business organization, you must now set out how much it will cost to get started, and what results you forecast for the first years of operation. There will be an Operating Budget, which is described under Budget, and a Start-Up Budget.

The Start-Up Budget forecasts in detail all expenditure needed to get the doors open for the first time, and, like all budgets, should be in the same format as the Accounts, so that as expenditures are incurred, forecast and performance can be accurately compared, ensuring tight financial control from the start. It will, however, be much more detailed than the Operating Budget for two reasons: first, this start-up expenditure represents investment which has to be justified, and secondly, just like an Antarctic expedition, you will need a checklist of equipment. You will have quite enough worries on opening day without suddenly finding that there are no scissors at the giftwrap table, or pens at the cash register. It might be said that such detail does not belong in the Business Plan, but it has to form part of the preparation, and it pays to include it as a sub-section or schedule, where it may not be studied, but will certainly show that you have done your homework, and have not made any vague estimates.

In the Operating Budget, this sort of expenditure will not be itemized, but will simply be included under the appropriate heading, such as Office Supplies, and control will be exercised by comparing monthly expenditure with the budgeted amount, but in the Start-Up Budget, for the reasons given, you need to itemize exactly what Office Expenditure, and all other categories, consist of.

The final items in the Business Plan will be your own resume and personal financial statement. Even if, or perhaps especially if, you are financing the entire enterprise yourself, make out a full personal financial statement and go over it as if you were a banker with indigestion.

You may or may not decide to include your resume in the initial presentation of the Business Plan, depending upon whom you are approaching, but have it ready; it will almost certainly be required sooner or later. In any case the preparation of a resume, if you have not done it before, or not at least for some considerable time, can be very instructive, and surprisingly helpful in achieving the aim of Robert Burns:

> "O wad some Pow'r the giftie gie us
> To see oursels as others see us!
> It wad frae mony a blunder free us
> And foolish notion."

BUYING A BUSINESS: Do not buy a business in which you have no experience. Apart from the obvious pitfalls, prospective lenders and investors will almost certainly want to see your resume, and if it includes no relevant, or preferably specific, experience, you will find it doubly hard to persuade them.

If you do come fresh into a new business, learn its bookkeeping and accounting language. The fundamental principles of Sales, cost of goods sold, and expenses are standard, but the language of a manufacturing plant, for instance, is different from that of a retail store. I have seen a brilliant manufacturing executive floundering because he tried to fit the manufacturing category of "materials" into a retail setting, where it does not fit, and gets confused with "inventory." He took an expensively long time to adjust to the fact that inventory was simply merchandise, and that there were no separate materials and finished products.

This again has its effect on lenders and investors. A Business Plan for a retail store couched in manufacturing language will not create a good impression on a prospective lender who is familiar with retailing.

It goes without saying that you must be satisfied with the financial condition of the business you are buying. Sadly, a mere examination of the records may not be enough: they need to be verified. I have seen a business bought in good faith, but which was soon afterwards dunned for debts which had been falsely shown as paid.

There is no firm formula for establishing the value of a business. Obviously its earnings during previous years will be the major factor, but the owner may feel that it is worth to him, after many years of effort, more than the figures indicate, and he may prefer to carry on rather than sell. Again, previous profits may not be sustainable if the local business atmosphere has changed: a new mall may be under construction nearby, or the building may have changed hands, causing renewal of the lease on favorable terms to be a problem.

Goodwill is particularly difficult to evaluate, or even to define. It can be said to have no separate value at all, as its existence will be reflected in the financial success of the business. It can perhaps, however, be identified as the value of a name. An owner may agree to sell everything except the name, with the buyer free to continue without interruption in the same premises. If the name was included, the price would probably be higher, and thus equivalent to Goodwill. It might, of course happen that the name has become tarnished in the public mind, and the buyer would be better off changing it. Goodwill then would hardly be an issue.

Take into account the physical condition of the premises, such as the age and condition of the air conditioning system, the state of the floor, and the costs of any remodeling which you may feel necessary. With that in mind, check the terms of the Lease, and make a point of meeting the landlord as soon as negotiations with the owner make this possible.

Lastly, the overriding factor in buying a business, apart from the money available, is your own motivation. Cold-blooded assessment of return on investment is not sufficient unless you aim to install a professional manager. If you intend to run the business yourself, as a full-time owner, you must want to do it for its own sake, because it is something which you will enjoy. *See* Motivation.

©The Wall Street Journal, used with permission

Well, what did you *expect* a Financial Wizard to look like?

C

CALL CARDS. In a perfect world you would never be out of stock of anything, but in real life you will disappoint customers because you are waiting for a shipment. This can be turned almost to advantage by using Call Cards, showing the customer's name, address, telephone number and needs. The cards are filed by vendor, to be pulled when the next order is placed (or with it if already outstanding), so the vendor's name, not the customer's, must be at the top. The Purchase Order should be cross-referenced to the Call Card, and the customer is called when the goods come in.

The advantage of this system is not only that it gets the customer what she wants, but also that it impresses her enormously when she is called, and you get a reputation for exceptional service.

The customer should not fill out the Call Card herself, as her writing may be illegible. In any case the cards need to be in standard form, and she will probably put things in the wrong places. (*See also* Special Orders and the Appendix, p. 190.)

CAPITAL. The single word always needs to be qualified: there are Start-Up Capital, Working Capital, and Invested Capital.

Start-up Capital is not a technical accounting term. It will simply become Working Capital and Capital when the business is running. It is, however, the usual term for the lump sum needed to start a new business, for the purchase of furniture, fixtures and fittings, for re-modeling and for opening inventory, and for lease, telephone and utility deposits, plus provision for operating expenses for the first year, or until the business is at least self-sustaining. *See* Financing a Business.

Working Capital: A business cannot prosper if it lives on sales receipts from day to day, any more than an individual can prosper living from paycheck to paycheck. There must always be Working Capital available for purchasing inventory and for expenses. Lack of Working Capital is one of the primary causes of business failure.

In a new business it will consist of the surviving cash and inventory (Current Assets) portion of the start-up Capital, after paying for the furniture, fixtures, and fittings etc., mentioned above. It pays all operating (*i.e.* working) costs, including merchandise replenishment.

Working Capital in a going concern is properly defined as Current Assets (Cash, Accounts Receivable and Inventory) less Current Liabilities (Accounts Payable and Monthly Expenses). It can be expressed in dollars, or as a Ratio (Current Assets divided by Current Liabilities). The Ratio is best for year to year comparisons, as it is independent of actual dollar volume. It should never, of course, be less than One (Current Assets less than Current Liabilities).

If Inventory is selling slowly, not producing cash flow, and thus not truly deserving of the name "current" asset, you may choose to leave it out of the calculation, if you simply need to assess the immediate cash position.

A hidden aspect of Working Capital is the time difference between buying goods on thirty day credit, and selling them for cash. Imagine buying $1,000 worth of goods on thirty day credit, and selling them at Keystone ($2,000) for cash. Thirty days' sales will (or certainly should) generate enough to pay most or all of the purchase price, but if you had had to pay c.o.d., or send Cash With Order, Working Capital will be reduced. This emphasizes, once again, the critical importance of maintaining good credit with your vendors.

Invested Capital is a part, with Retained Earnings, of Owner's Equity. It is the sum originally invested, subject to increase or decrease according to the fortunes of the business. On the Liabilities side of a Balance Sheet you might see (with more detail) this sort of arrangement:

A:	Current Liabilities	10,000
	Long Term Liabilities	+ 20,000
	Total Liabilities	**30,000**
B:	Owner's Equity (his original investment)	**50,000**
C:	Retained Earnings from last month	10,000
	Loss this month	– 3,000
	Retained Earnings this month	**7,000**
	Total Liabilities (A+B+C)	**87,000**

This half Balance Sheet (Assets are omitted) shows that from this month's operations $7,000 were retained and added to the owner's original investment of $50,000. "Retained," however, is the right word, for it was all that was retained from the $10,000 of the previous month after deducting this month's loss of $3,000.

The account is in balance because Owner's Equity and Retained Earnings equal the difference between the Assets and the Short and Long Term Liabilities, or between what is owned and what is owed. The apparently contradictory presence of Retained Earnings and Owner's Equity on the Liabilities side is explained by the fact that they are owed by the business to the owner.

CAR. An ordinary retail store does not need a company car. If you or your staff have to run errands, keep a mileage log and reimburse at the standard rate approved by the IRS. Very inexpensive insurance is available to cover accidents involving privately owned cars on company business. If there are compelling reasons for the business to run a car or van, consider the competing advantages of purchase and of lease. Purchase, of course, is a Capital item, with its Depreciation as an Expense, while lease is wholly an Expense. The choice will depend on your particular circumstances: consult your accountant.

CASH. You will need a cash float in the cash register, some petty cash, in a cash box in the office (unless you pay petty cash amounts from the register – *see* Petty Cash), and some reserve cash to make change for the cashier as necessary: one or two customers with $50 or $100 bills early in the day can play havoc with the float in the register. How much you allow for each of these will depend on the scale of your business: perhaps $150 in coin and bills in the Register, the same again in reserve, and $100 Petty Cash.

It is bad practice, and inviting muddle, to make Petty Cash payments out of the Cash Register, unless the bookkeeping is computerized, in which case petty cash expenditures can be made direct from the register, and posted to the appropriate account in the computer with the rest of the day's transactions.

CASH FLOW. The meaning of this depends upon who is talking. I have seen a textbook in which one chart shows Monthly Cash Flow as cash on hand at the start and end of the month, taking into account the month's sales, expenses, etc., while another chart in the same book starts with pre-tax income, and defines Cash Flow in two ways; as "operating – the cash generated in a year," or "free – a measure of a stock's value." For day-to-day management, which is our concern here, we need the Monthly Cash Flow, comparing performance to Forecast.

Cash is very appropriately called a Liquid Asset. It needs to flow through the business in a steady stream, the steadier the better, and a Cash Flow Forecast enables you to control it.

Cash comes from one source, and one source only – *sales* – but flows to many needs: Accounts Payable (whatever else you may owe, Accounts Payable refers only to monthly bills, mainly merchandise); expenses; Wages and Salaries; Debt Service and Taxes. These will fall due weekly, bimonthly, monthly, quarterly, and annually. Build them accurately into the cash flow forecast. Do not, for instance, spread a quarterly payment into a monthly average. Place it precisely in the months concerned, so that the cash will be there.

A good Cash Flow Forecast disciplines your daily management. It shows you, for instance, how to space your Purchase Orders (or at least the delivery dates) so that a bunch placed at a Trade Show will not all arrive at once, with all the payments falling due with a combined thud.

This enables you to keep Accounts Payable current, which not only protects your all-important credit, but ensures that the flow of goods is not disrupted by the delays of "Credit Hold." This can cause a logjam until payments are up-to-date, when all outstanding orders will be delivered at once, with a consequent surge in Payables which may be difficult to meet, and you will be back on Credit Hold again. This does not do the Cash Flow any good at all.

Whenever possible, order little and often, within the limits of economical freight, and vendors' special deals, discounts, and minimums.

To maintain maximum Cash Flow, make sure that no cash is sitting around unused, in the shape of outdated or unsaleable inventory. This needs to be sold off at reduced prices, and the cash used on new inventory that will get the flow going again. Better to have $10 cash working for you than a $20 item unsold for a year.

A substantial percentage of the Cash Flow is diverted into Sales Tax. This can cause problems if one thinks of Cash Flow in terms of the amount deposited in the bank, because you are a mere tax collector for the State. If, for instance, the tax rate is 8%, and the day's bank deposit is $1,000, only $925.93 will be yours. Make sure that the Cash Flow Forecast shows Net Sales.

CASH FLOW	January Actual	January Budget	% ±
Cash on Hand, first of month	5,342.00	5,000.00	+7%
Sales	24,358.00	25,000.00	–3%
Other Income (*specify*)			
A: Total Month's Cash	29,700.00	30,000.00	–1%
B: Purchases, Merchandise	13,397.00	13,750.00	–3%
Expenses			
Advertising			
Auto … (*full list as Income Statement*)			
C: Total Month's Expenses	9,744.00	10,000.00	–3%
Non-Operating Expenditure			
Loan Capital Repaid (*Interest will be in Expenses*)	2,000.00	2,000.00	
Capital Purchases			
Owner's draw	350.00	350.00	
Employee Loans			
Other			
D: Total Non-Op Expenditure	2,350.00	2,350.00	
Cash On Hand, end of month (*A -B -C -D*)	4,209.00	3,900.00	+8%

Although this looks very like the Net Income Statement, cost of goods sold is replaced by Purchases, Merchandise, and Cash on Hand,and some non-expense items are included which do not appear on the Income Statement. It does exactly what its name implies: it compares the monthly flow of actual cash with forecast income and requirements.

It is not difficult to compile a Cash Flow Forecast by hand, but it is extremely tedious and time consuming. A computer is essential. You can use the Cash Flow facility in your bookkeeping software, but this will only extrapolate from past performance. For projections based on planned changes in performance, use the spreadsheet in your Microsoft Office™, Lotus Smart Suite™, or any other software of your choice.

CASH MANAGEMENT. If you are fortunate enough to have an occasional, seasonal, or regular cash surplus it is foolish to let it sit idle. Assuming that you do not want to expand operations or premises, increase your salary, pay dividends, or simply, if you are sole owner, take it home, you should consider how best to use it.

The obvious way is to put it in an interest-bearing account at your bank, topping up the checking account from it, or transferring overflow to it, as circumstances permit. This, however, is only one of many possible suggestions. The important thing, with so many opportunities in today's versatile financial world, is not to let the horse stand idle in the stable, but to put it to work.

It is more difficult, but even more important, to manage a cash shortage. It cannot be done without a Cash Flow Forecast, a Budget and full accounts. These will give you not only complete details of how much is owed to whom, and when, but also a soundly based forecast by which to plan remedial action. This is not only essential if you have to apply for a loan, but it also puts you in a stronger position to negotiate special arrangements with individual creditors or, in the case of particularly "squeaky wheels," pay out of turn. The golden rule is: Always respond to your creditors, even if you cannot pay on time. Hell hath no fury like a credit manager ignored.

As mentioned under Time Management, just as a well-organized and tidy closet has more useable space than a messy one, so well-organized Cash Management frees up more useable cash.

CASH REGISTER. The original, and still the main function of the Cash Register is simply to record the amount of cash and other forms of payment which have been received during the day, so that at close of business the actual amounts received (cash, checks, credit card payments) can be checked against the register's print-out. This ensures that what is deposited in the bank is the exact amount of what was actually sold, and if you employ a cashier it is also a safeguard against theft.

Basic registers of this type are still available, some with a considerable array of buttons for different types of merchandise, and various methods of payment, but the modern Cash Register is fast becoming a specialized computer which does a great deal more, either independently, or as part of a store network, and is fully discussed under Computers (*which see*).

A security tip: leave empty registers open at night, so that thieves will not do expensive damage breaking into them.

CASHIER. The cashier will often be the first person the customer sees when she enters the store, the last person she sees when she leaves, and perhaps the only person she has spoken to while there. However fine the quality of your merchandise and the brilliance of your display, it will be the quality of that human contact that will leave the most lasting impression in the customer's mind.

This will be particularly true in the many small stores where cashiers are primarily sales people, spending as much time out on the floor with customers, or seeing to the displays, as at the register. In that situation, the cashier must be very sensitive to customers' movements, so that nobody is kept waiting at the register. To the customer, fifteen seconds being ignored at an unattended register is a very long time; quite enough, sometimes, to lose a sale and cause a swift, bad-tempered exit. The customer is, of course, being unreasonable, but catering to the whims of unreasonable people goes with the territory.

Even where the cashier and sales functions are separate, it is essential that the cashier be not only courteous (one of the worst crimes a cashier can commit is to talk to a colleague while checking out a customer), but also fully trained as a sales person, because whoever else may be absent, the cashier will always be there. Nothing is more infuriating to a customer than to find nobody to answer her questions except the cashier, who then turns out to know nothing about the merchandise.

Cashiers are the front-line troops of retailing. There may be no owner, manager or supervisor in the store, but there will always be a cashier, who, apart from the qualities described above, will also have to know how to deal with a multitude of problems, from difficult customers to armed robbery. Give your cashier written instructions on how to deal with any eventuality. If, for instance, a customer wants to return something without a receipt, the cashier must be able to refer to written policy, which should be so phrased that it can be shown to the customer if things get difficult (although the cashier must be free to use her best judgment in extreme situations). Likewise, if a customer comes in to redeem a bounced check, the cashier must know where the returned check is, and must know exactly what procedure to follow in accepting or rejecting the customer's redemption. Written instructions not only relieve the cashier of unfair burdens, but also ensure that all customers are served efficiently and consistently.

In addition to all this, the cashier must be able to keep a cool head, ringing up sales and making change accurately, even while distracted by customers' questions.

Armed robbery hardly requires any rules. Simply tell your cashier to "give him the money, obey him quickly, and look at him as little as possible, so he won't think you are memorizing his appearance."

The telephone should never be allowed to disrupt service to a customer. If the cashier has to answer it she must give the customer priority, and should either put the caller on hold, offer to call back, call another member of the staff, or transfer the call to the office. Training will be needed to ensure that this is done with courtesy and speed, because the caller may, of course, also be a customer.

The cashier has one of the most difficult jobs in retailing, and deserves all the support you can give. The personality of your cashier can be, in large part, the public's perception of the personality of your store. She is your front-line representative.

CASHING OUT. *See* Reconciling the Register.

CHAIRS. Some for the office, of course, and for relaxation with a cup of coffee in the back, and one up front for the cashier, but do also have a chair or two out in the showroom where the elderly, the infirm and the just plain tired can sit and rest, or consult a shopping list, or look up a telephone number. If your store includes books, chairs are a virtual necessity for dedicated browsers (they'll buy in the end). In any case, you should provide for grandfather, in order to free the family to shop at leisure while he rests.

Other things being equal, customers will come to the store which provides the best in courtesy and comfort.

CHANGE: *see* Float.

CHARGE ACCOUNTS. However simple a Charge Account system may be, it will still cost money to run, and you lose some working capital – the difference between cash on the barrel-head at the cash register, and the 30-day open account you have with your vendors. There will also be some bad debts, which not only cost you money, but can lead to unnecessary bad feeling between you and your customers unless tactfully handled.

On the other hand, Charge Accounts make loyal customers, who will bring repeat business, and as you must any way send out monthly Statements, you can offset the cost, and perhaps do more, by enclosing some advertising. Many vendors offer attractive sales brochures specifically designed as "statement stuffers," which can be overprinted with your store name at very little cost. A fundamental gain is that every month you actively encourage your customers to come in, rather than passively wait for them.

The success of Charge Accounts depends on efficiency. If they are well run, with the minimum of complaints and queries from the customers, all will be well. If they are badly run, they will not only lose you money, but also reputation, and do more harm than good.

CHARITY. You and your business are as much part of the community as are your customers. Participate as much as you can, although there will be times when you feel you are being virtually blackmailed by "go-getters," who make barely veiled threats about loss of goodwill, and specious statements about the generosity of your competitors. A good defense is to keep a diary of every solicitation you receive, with a note of the donation, if any. If you can show that you have already had three requests that week, even the most hardened go-getter will relent – and do not forget that the hard approach may be an over-reaction from a basic shyness. Many of those who come to you are doing so more from duty than pleasure.

Whenever you are approached, make sure that the request is for a genuine non-profit organization, so that your contribution will be tax-deductible, and get a formal receipt on the organization's printed form.

You will get a considerable number of telephone solicitations. You can either say that you do not accept telephone requests, or ask the caller to send details in the mail.

CHART OF ACCOUNTS: Income, Expenses, Liabilities and Assets are different types of Account, within which are individual accounts such as Sales (an Income account), Advertising (an Expense account), Loans payable (a Liability account) or Accounts Receivable (an Asset account). Each of these types of Account will have a separate range of numbers, with an individual number for each category. Expenses, for instance, might be allocated the 6000 range, with Advertising at 6000, Automobile Expense 6010, and so on. The numbers are spaced so that additions can be fitted in sequence. The Chart of Accounts is simply a classified list of all accounts. Computer accounting programs, such as Quickbooks™, have built in generic Charts of Accounts, which can be tailored to individual needs.

Much bookkeeping software is very good, but claims that you need no expertise to use it are exaggerated. It may indeed be easy to use, but only if you already know to which account a particular transaction belongs. Advertising, for instance, is obviously an Expense, and anyway is listed by name in the Chart of Accounts, so there is no problem in entering its account number when writing a check, but the proper classification of capital equipment, leasehold improvements, and other expenditures which are not expenses may not be so obvious, and the answer will not be in the software manual. A quick phone call to your CPA will solve the problem, particularly if he is familiar, as he should be, with your particular Chart of Accounts, and such calls will build your expertise to the point when they are seldom necessary.

CHARTER. If you form a Corporation, it will have a Corporate Charter. This defines the purposes of the corporation, and use of corporate funds must be confined to those purposes. For a small private corporation, such as we are discussing, the Charter will probably be a very simple, if not standard, document. On the next page is a typical form. See the appropriate bureau in your state for guidelines and necessary forms.

CHECK BOOK: Business checks come in many forms, and it is worth some trouble to find out what is available and what will best suit your personal requirements, and those of the business. The choice of carbon copies or check stubs with a separate register is personal, while the layout of the voucher will depend upon the business. It is convenient, for instance, if you do payroll, to have check vouchers laid out to show Gross Wages, itemized Deductions, Net Pay, etc., but which also have space to show vendors' Invoice numbers when paying for merchandise.

The check book is one of the most frequently used tools on your workbench. Like any other tool, it will cause much irritation and shoddy work if it is not carefully selected to suit its owner and its purpose.

ARTICLES OF INCORPORATION

Article One

The name of the corporation is ________________. (Must contain Company, Corporation, Incorporated or an abbreviation thereof.)

Article Two

The period of duration is perpetual. (May be for a number of years or until a date certain.)

Article Three

The purpose for which the corporation is organized is the transaction of any and all lawful business for which corporations may be incorporated under the Texas Business Corporation Act. (Specific purposes may be stated).

Article Four

The aggregate number of shares which the corporation shall have authority to issue is ________of the par value of __________ Dollars ($_____) each. (Shares may be of no par value.)

Article Five

The corporation will not commence business until it has received for the issuance of shares consideration of the value of One Thousand Dollars ($1,000.00) consisting of money, labor done or property actually received.

Article Six

The street address of its initial registered office is ____________, and the name of its initial registered agent at such address is __________. (Use the street, building or rural route address of the registered office; a post office box number is not sufficient.)

Article Seven

The number of directors constituting the initial board of directors is ______, and the names and addresses of the person or persons who are to serve as directors until the first annual meeting of the shareholders or until their successors are elected and qualified are:

Article Eight

The name(s) and address(es) of the incorporator(s) is(are):

(signed)

_________________________________ Incorporator(s)

If you have a computer program for bookkeeping, use it to the full and print out the checks. Again, several types are available, so select with care, preferably from the software company itself, so that everything will be compatible. Having the computer print the checks also ensures that they get into the program's check register, which may sometimes get missed if they are hand-written.

CHECK REGISTER: The successful owner always knows exactly how much money is available. Keep the Check Register current daily, and reconcile the Bank Statement promptly every month. If you were the CEO of a large corporation, what would you think of the manager of a subsidiary who could not tell you immediately the current bank balance? *See* Reconciling the Register.

CHRISTMAS. There is hardly any type of retail store that does not feel the surge of the Christmas tide. Many gift shops merely tread water for the first eleven months of the year (often with the help of a life-preserving bridging loan from the bank), and are swept onto the safe shores of profit only in December.

Whatever the effect of Christmas on your store, watch for lucrative vendors' offers early in the year, for there may be some that expire as early as the end of March. This early cut-off probably means that the vendor intends to import or manufacture only the quantities for which he then has orders, so you are faced with a now-or-never decision.

At the other extreme, some vendors advertise that during the Christmas season they guarantee to ship all orders within 24 hours, which saves you a lot of anxious forecasting. This, of course, only applies if your credit is good, so make sure, if cash is tight, that at least these accounts are kept up-to-date.

Between these two extremes, there will be early-booking discounts, or deferred-billing offers, or reduced-price package deals, or any one of a multitude of other temptations which vendors devise to enrich themselves, and which will also, if you order carefully, enrich you. Whatever you do about special offers, you have to make the best sales forecast you can, as early as you can. Project your cash flow, and place orders accordingly, with the ship dates carefully staggered, so that the goods arrive when needed, your back-room does not get physically overwhelmed, and you do not have to pay for everything at once.

Keep some Christmas merchandise on display all year: customers may not buy it in June, but when they are ready they will know where to come. Quite a small display will do; just enough to convey the message. There is nothing worse than to hear a Christmas customer say "I wish I had known you carried that. I went all the way to Blumps yesterday to get some." (But even worse is the one who says "I wish I had heard of you a month ago. I would have done all my Christmas shopping here," but that is an advertising problem.)

You will of course decorate the store – it will make people feel "Christmasy," and in the mood to buy gifts, or treats for themselves – but don't do it too early. Customers can be quite offended if they feel you are pushing too hard and "commercializing Christmas." On the other hand, you will be amazed at the number of Summer customers who ask when the Christmas merchandise will be coming in. There will even be some who ask when you are going to have your post-Christmas sale, having done their shopping for this Christmas in last January's sales.

You may need an extra cash register during the Christmas season. Long lines at the Register are certainly encouraging, but they look better from the merchant's point of view than from the customer's, and a good way of keeping things moving is to use a second Register as the Express Lane – cash only and no giftwrap. Quick and courteous service is good for your reputation, and never more so than at Christmas time, when so many customers are coming in for the first time. A well-managed Christmas should not only be very profitable in itself, but should also add substantially to your regular customer base.

CLAIMS. For shipments by common carrier damage claims usually lie between the consignee (you) and the trucking company. UPS, on the other hand, will reimburse the shipper, your vendor, but it is up to you to give both of them the details. UPS will reimburse your vendor, who in turn will reimburse you.

It may seem a waste of time to claim for one small breakage in a shipment, and certainly some insurance companies seem to want to encourage that attitude, judging by their fussy and over-detailed claim forms, which often ask for more information than can possibly fit in the space provided.

Do claim, though, for all damage, and make sure that word gets back to the shipper, whose bad packing is usually the cause. Many vendors enclose instructions for damage claims in the shipment, and it is wise to follow them. In some cases all that is needed is a call to the sales rep., who may have the authority to issue a credit memo.

Sometimes when the value is small, if you send the trucking company a copy of the invoice showing exactly what was damaged and the cost, with a cover letter pointing out that the claim is too small to justify a formal claim, they may settle at once.

Shipping damage is rarely a major problem in individual shipments, but the cumulative effect can substantially erode profits. To keep this to a minimum, ride herd on all claims, large and small, and set up receiving procedures that will make absolutely sure that all details are noted on the documents and are followed through into bookkeeping and inventory control.

CLOCKING ON. The time-clock is not a symbol of the capitalist exploitation of the downtrodden worker. On the contrary, if you have hourly and part-time workers it is the best way to give them the most flexible and convenient working hours. It eliminates disputes about hours worked, or wages owed, and keeps track of special time off and of overtime. It saves employees the trouble of keeping a record of their own hours, and the cards are more legible than a signing-in book.

A time-clock is particularly useful if you use Employee Leasing (*which see*), as it ensures that hours worked are always to hand, and the deadline for sending them to the leasing company will not be missed.

C.I.F. Usually in lower case – c.i.f. – stands for Carriage Insurance and Freight. More commonly used in international shipments, it means that the vendor will pay all those delivery costs. If your store were in Houston, for instance, "c.i.f. Houston" would mean that all those charges would be paid to Houston Airport or docks, although you would still have to pay the small delivery charge from there to the store. For domestic shipments you will more often see "fgt. pd.," which will get the shipment right to your door. *See also* F.O.B.

CLOSE-OUTS. Beware of tempting close-out prices offered by vendors on items which they have discontinued. A good item may be discontinued simply because its regular price is too high and the vendor cannot afford to reduce it; the close-out prices then may earn you a nice profit, but some items are close-outs because they are unsaleable at any price. Do not go for a close-out offer just because it seems to be an irresistible bargain.

C.O.D. Cash on Delivery. Your first order or two from a new vendor will probably be sent C.O.D., unless you choose to wait while the vendor checks your credit references, which you will have sent with the order. You will also be put on C.O.D. status if your account gets too delinquent. The disadvantages of C.O.D. are, first, that you do not have the usual thirty days in which to sell at least some of the goods before you have to pay for them, and secondly, freight costs can be inflated by an extra C.O.D. charge. The only advantage of C.O.D. is that it is better than C.W.O., Cash With Order, where you pay for the goods long before you get them, and even then, you may not get all you paid for. C.O.D. is acceptable, or at least bearable when necessary, but C.W.O. should be avoided.

COCKPIT CHECK. Just as a pilot makes sure that all is well before flight, so must you ensure that before opening for business each morning, the floor is clean, displays are dusted, checked and refreshed, the cashier is fully equipped with merchandise bags, pens, credit memos, a full stapler, spare cash register tape, telephone message pad, eraser, scotch tape, Kleenex etc. A bright clean store and smooth, speedy operation at the register are among the most effective image-boosters for the store. *See* Daily Duties.

COFFEE BREAK. If you possibly can, set aside a "lunch room" in the back with a coffee maker, refrigerator, sink, dishwasher and microwave, so that you and your staff can enjoy an uninterrupted lunch or coffee break in comfort. It makes all the difference to everyone's staying power and morale, particularly if there is real cream in the refrigerator, and people bring their own mugs, rather than having milk powder and plastic cups. The whole point will be lost, however, if the lunch room is not kept clean and tidy. Responsibilities for this must be clearly defined.

A particular advantage of this arrangement is that it enables you to enforce what should be an absolutely unbreakable rule against carrying coffee cups into the showroom, where the atmosphere should be one of friendly professionalism, not sloppy informality.

COLLATERAL: It is virtually impossible to borrow money without offering Collateral (unless you have remarkably accommodating relatives or friends). In private arrangements the amount is, of course, negotiable, but commercially you may be asked for collateral amounting to about two-thirds of the loan, with one third in cash and one third in assets. At least be ready for this, even though the lender may, in the event, ask for less. *See* Financing a Business.

COMMISSIONS: *see* Incentives.

COMPARISONS: WEEKLY & MONTHLY, ACTUAL VS. TARGET. Running a business is like firing a gun: you need a target. A chart showing actual performance against weekly and monthly targets is easily made and maintained if you have a spreadsheet program such as Excel™ or Lotus 1-2-3™ in your computer. A sample is shown in the Appendix, p. 200.

COMPETITORS: Be aware of, but do not fear, competition. Always assume that you lead and others follow. Leadership, in this context, does not simply mean underselling other merchants: it means that you offer the most attractive merchandise, the best service, and the best value for money. Adjust your inventory to take account, for instance, of a discount house underselling you on a particular line of merchandise, but do not assume that you will never sell any of it at full price again. Do not worry, either, about similar stores nearby. London's Charing Cross Road is a mass of bookstores, and their numbers make it a destination for book lovers. Even if a near neighbor carries virtually identical merchandise, your store's efficiency, service, attractive decor and reputation will keep you ahead.

You may still complain to the sales rep if a line which you carry appears for the first time in a neighboring merchant's window, but his reasons for selling to them may give you food for thought, such as perhaps a gradual decline in your volume of business with him which you had overlooked, indicating the need for some changes on your part to remedy the situation.

COMPLAINTS: The soft answer turneth away wrath. If a customer brings back an item with a complaint, clear the air first by asking (unless it is obvious) "Did you get it here?" and secondly "How long ago?"

If the answers are reasonable, offer replacement, credit memo, or cash refund. This virtually unconditional offer will gain far more than any dollar saved by rejecting the complaint, even if you do not feel it is justified.

COMPUTERS. BC (Before Computers) calculators merely scratched the surface of business, just as primitive plows just scratched the surface of the earth. The metal plowshare changed that – the computer likewise has changed business. Do not ever think of it as a mere labor-saving gadget. It digs deeper than any calculator ever could, and releases the full productive potential of your business.

If you can afford to go first class, invest in a fully integrated system. It will incorporate continuous Inventory Control, and can therefore produce all the bookkeeping and management data you could ask for, including "real time" (*which see*) Net Income Statements (which require inventory data for the critical Cost of Goods Sold). Such a system consists of a POS (Point of Sale) computer with cash drawer – *i.e.* a computerized Cash Register – connected to an office computer, the whole running on built-in software which will produce complete up-to-date reports on every aspect of the business at the drop of a hat.

Data entry, of course, particularly for inventory, must itself be up-to-date, and as far as the Cash Register is concerned always will be, because as items are sold they are automatically deducted from Inventory. In order for there to be any Inventory to be deducted from, however, all merchandise must be entered into the system when received. This is not by any means automatic, and calls for thorough preparation and discipline, but is much easier and simpler than it used to be, now that most items are already bar coded (with codes easily generated for the few that are not), and scanners readily affordable.

Integrated systems will not to be found in the mass market computer stores, but are offered as complete packages by specialist vendors. They can be very impressive, but it is easy to spend a great deal of money on a fine system that is completely unsuitable for your particular needs. It is essential to put those needs in writing, as specifications for the software performance, before you go shopping. The bookkeeping end will probably present little problem, as the final form of Net Income Statement, Balance Sheet, etc., is fairly standard. Questions may arise, however, at the Cash Register, where there may be more types of transaction than the software designers – or you – had expected (and bookkeeping will indeed have to accommodate them).

The list below shows the remarkable variety of transactions which occur in a typical small retail store. Have the Cash Register programmed to deal with your specific requirements, and if it cannot cope with come of them, the cashier should have a simple form for each, so that the necessary adjustments can be made when Reconciling the Register (*which see*).

Payment received for:	Straight sale	
	Goods on Consignment	
	Lay-Away deposit or installment	
	Lay-Away final pay-out	
	Special Order deposit	
	Special Order payment on delivery	
	Bad check redemption	
By:	Cash	
	Check	
	Traveler's Check	
	Credit Card:	American Express, Visa , MasterCard, Discover (each keyed in separately)
	Credit Memo for goods returned	
	Gift Certificate	
Money or Credit given for:	Returns	
	Petty Cash:	(*e.g.* Window cleaning: with a computer it can be simpler to record such payments at the register than to have a Petty Cash box and account).
	Overcharges	
Discounts given for:	Store Sales	
	Vendors' promotions	
	Staff privileges	
Value of merchandise or Gift Certificate donated for Charity.		

Even with an integrated system, you will still need a standard office PC, preferably with at least 16 megabytes of RAM and a high capacity hard disk (a less powerful machine will be adequate, but will work slowly, be frustrating, and cost you valuable time), for correspondence, spreadsheet planning, mail order database, store signs, advertising copy, brochure and newsletter composition, or whatever.

This computer, loaded with off-the-shelf bookkeeping software such as Peachtree™ or Quickbooks™, can also do all that an integrated system can do, except automatically produce a Net Income Statement, because it does not have the necessary inventory figures. The programs do have inventory control but, being designed primarily for manufacturing or service industries, every sale is assumed to be on a program-generated invoice, which does the deduction from inventory. In retail, sales are recorded in the Cash Register, and so not invoiced, and not deducted from inventory. The day's receipts for these sales can be entered into the PC's Check Register, but this will not itemize methods of payment (let alone all the variations listed above). All this can be solved easily, and the programs mentioned will give excellent results, but it requires a little homework, and some help, perhaps from a CPA who is familiar with the software.

If, however, the cash register is an independent POS computer, it will maintain full Inventory Control, by deducting every sale as it occurs (goods received are entered by scanning in bar codes), so inventory is available whenever needed for a Net Income Statement. This POS computer also provides complete transaction analysis which can readily be keyed into the office PC for day-to-day bookkeeping as comprehensive as on an integrated system.

In addition to keeping track of mere quantities of inventory, the POS computer, whether independent or integrated, maintains purchasing history and sales performance of every item, and much other valuable data unrelated to bookkeeping. It will tell you, for instance, not only how many Gizmos and Widgets are in stock, but also how many pink Gizmos have been sold in the past three months, or year, or whatever period you chose. To have the sales history of any item available at any time is obviously of immense value, as all deadwood can readily be identified and culled from inventory, and future purchasing accurately planned.

The POS Computer can also keep detailed buying analysis on individual customers, showing who has bought what, in what quantity, and when, which is, of course, essential information for profitable direct mail and other advertising.

There is not room here to describe all the valuable features of the POS Computer, for which the best source (as an independent unit) is probably an established cash register business which has kept fully up-to-date and become, in effect, a computer dealer specializing in the needs of the retail trade.

Bearing in mind that anything said here may well be out of date at any moment, the suggestions for a small retail store are thus either the fully integrated system, plus an office PC, or simply an office PC plus an independent computerized Cash Register.

If you are not at ease with computers, or need help in choosing a program, it is very helpful to take classes, which are often available from the School District or the Community College, and from private organizations and computer stores. It is easier to choose hardware than software: the full capabilities of the hardware can be determined before purchase, but it is seldom possible to try out a software program. You have to rely on word-of-mouth recommendations, newspaper articles, manuals, and, for some programs, independent books.

CONSIGNMENT. If you accept goods On Consignment, you do not pay for them until they are sold, which is very desirable, but is an arrangement seldom offered by trade vendors, and then only on a specific line of merchandise. If it is offered, be sure to keep very accurate records from the beginning, to ensure that you pay for no more (and no less) than you have sold. Do not rely on the vendor's sales representative to do the periodic inventory check for you, unless you cross-check at the same time. If you do not, and find later that a mistake has been made, it may be difficult to put things right.

You may get requests from private individuals to accept items for them on Consignment. If this suits your store it may well be profitable, adding unique and attractive items to your inventory at no cost, but again be very sure to keep accurate records.

Both with trade vendors and particularly with private individuals, make sure that all financial details are agreed before accepting the merchandise.

Items on consignment remain the property of the consignor, so should not be taken into inventory. If they are included in a computerized Inventory Control program, care must be taken to ensure that data and transactions are recorded without affecting inventory value.

CONSTIPATION: A business can suffer two forms of constipation: physical and financial. The physical form is caused by too much inventory in too little space. Much of it will of necessity be inadequately displayed, will not, therefore, move through the system as fast as it could, and will not produce that essential fertilizer for success, money. Every store has a maximum Yield per Square Foot, which can only be determined by experience. When you find that stuffing in more inventory does not increase that yield, you will know that the business is constipated. The cause, of course, may not be entirely lack of space; it may also be bad diet, but so long as you are confident that you are buying the right merchandise, then space is the problem.

Even with plenty of space, the store may still suffer from Financial Constipation. It is no good buying a load of widgets at a fabulous discount if the minimum order gives you a year's supply, or if you consistently buy more than the store can easily digest. Your money will all be stuck in the bowels of the back-room when it should be being spread about fertilizing the showroom with well-judged quantities of fast-selling merchandise.

COPY MACHINE: Efficiency will suffer severely for lack of a copy machine. Vendors will provide single-copy order forms – if you want to use them, you must have a file copy. A customer may need a copy of a vendor's retail price list, and with a good copy machine you can not only provide one instantly, but also cut and paste your store name onto it. You can create a simple office form on the computer, such as the daily Cashing Out analysis, and run off a supply. On the computer, too, you can create attractive store signs, and announcements, or a complete store Brochure, and run off the quantities needed much more quickly and cheaply than you could print them. The copy machine is a necessity, not a luxury. It needs to have full zoom enlargement and reduction, and be able to take 11×17 paper, as well as letter and legal size. The cost of color capability can only be justified if there is much desk-top publishing to be done, such as brochures, newsletters, catalogs, mailers, etc. *See also* Scanner.

CORPORATION. It may or may not be a good idea to incorporate your business. In deciding whether or not to do so, consider Federal and State law, and the likely effects of incorporation on your personal circumstances, on the size and strength of your business, and on your plans for the future. Consult your accountant and your attorney.

A common misconception about incorporation is that it insulates you as an individual from personal liability. This is true, in the sense that you cannot be sued for debts incurred by the corporation in the way of trade, but if you want to take out a corporate bank loan, for instance, you will almost certainly be asked for both a personal and a corporate financial statement, and the loan will also carry your signature both as an individual and as an officer of the corporation.

The advantages of a corporation are that many vendors prefer to deal with a bona fide Corporation rather than with an individual, that you are insulated from its trade debts, and that you can raise capital by selling stock, which is particularly advantageous if you fall within the definition of a small corporation, when the legal requirements for selling stock may be looser than for larger concerns.

The disadvantages are that you have to obey certain rules and follow certain procedures to satisfy State and Federal law and the IRS, which you may find unduly restrictive or tedious. The details vary from State to State, and although, as mentioned above, special provisions sometimes allow small corporations to operate comparatively informally, beware of IRS requirements which may be more stringent than the parallel State law.

There are excellent books on this subject, readily available in the public library, and it is well worth while to read them before taking their invariable advice to consult your attorney. You will take up much less of his expensive time if you know what you are talking about when you go to see him.

COSTING: Costing is the calculation of the retail price of merchandise to yield a specific profit, or the calculation of profit on merchandise which is to be sold at the vendor's suggested retail price (s.r.p.). Profit is calculated from the True Delivered Cost (TDC) of an item, not from its bare wholesale price.

To save time, and for consistency from one delivery to another, it is convenient to adopt a standard multiplier for calculating Retail from Wholesale prices. Straight Keystone (twice cost), for instance, will only suffice if you pay no freight, and you may settle on a multiplier of 2.2 or 2.5 to achieve it. A multiplier of 2.2, for instance, will cover freight up to 10% of net cost, as in this example: the freight on a $100 invoice (for 20 items @ $5 each net) is $10, or 10%, so the TDC (True Delivered Cost) per item will be $5 + 10% = $5.50, giving a retail at Keystone of $5.50 × 2 = $11.00. The simple 2.2 × $5 gives the same

$11.00. Choice of multiplier will depend on average freight costs, which can only be determined by experience.

If the Costing is wrong, everything will be wrong. It will have the same effect on your profits as poisoning the wells would have on your cattle. Even (or especially) when using a standard multiplier, cost every Invoice as a matter of routine, to ensure that you are maintaining the desired Profit Margin.

The meaning of "Price," "Net," "List," etc., varies with the context, and you need to be sure that you and the salesperson are talking the same language. As with so many business terms, "correct" depends on who you are talking to. The meanings and variants given below are those I am used to.

Cost: A vague term. It can be the vendor's regular wholesale price, or TDC (True Delivered Cost).

Keystone: Trade jargon for 100% mark-up – doubling the Cost or TDC. Also a verb: when quoting a cost, the rep might say "most people usually keystone it."

List: the vendor's s.r.p. (suggested retail price). Many vendors invoice at List less discount. Those who do will usually publish a retail price list.

Margin: a percentage, short for Profit Margin. If TDC is $1, and Retail is $2, the Profit is half the Retail, so Margin is 50%. (Also confusingly used in reference to Gross Profit on the Income Statement. Gross Profit is the dollar amount after subtracting cost of goods sold from Sales, and Gross Margin, or just Margin, is that amount as a percentage of Sales).

Mark-Down: a percentage of the retail price. To mark down an item 10% is simply to reduce the retail by 10%

Mark-Up: also a percentage. If TDC is $1 and Retail is $2, the TDC has been marked up 100%.

Net, or **Net Cost:** A very versatile term of which the proper meaning is, I believe, the Wholesale price of an order after discount but before freight, but sometimes the opposite, for some people may take "Net Cost" or "Final Net" to mean what the whole Invoice will come to, including freight etc.

Sometimes, too, if an order qualifies for quantity discount, but contains some items excluded from the discount offer, it may be said that those items are "at net," *i.e.* at the regular wholesale price. As usual, in other words, the context decides the meaning.

Price: Can mean Wholesale (Cost) Price, or Retail Price. It is best to say Wholesale, Cost, or Retail, and not use Price alone.

Profit: the difference between TDC and Retail Price of the single item: usually a percentage of the retail, but can be in dollars.

Profit and Margin are virtually interchangeable; both are short for Profit Margin.

Retail: short for Retail Price: what you charge the customer.

TDC: True Delivered Cost to the store, allowing for all discounts, freight, etc.

Wholesale: The Wholesale price is the price at which you buy from the vendor. If the Invoice is At Net, it means the bare price per item, probably before considering any quantity discounts or suchlike, and certainly before considering freight. If the Invoice is at List, Wholesale will be the price after discount.

The Costing procedure

Always cost from the Invoice, not from a price list, which may be out-of-date, and will anyway probably state that prices are subject to change without notice, or will be those ruling at time of delivery. If freight is charged on the Invoice, TDC will be the Invoice total, but if you have paid the driver for "Freight Collect," make sure that you add the amount to the Invoice before you start costing.

The Invoice should show at minimum:

- A Date, Invoice Number, and your P.O. Number.
- It may also show the vendor's own Order Number, details of Terms (*e.g. 2/10, Net 30*).
- A Customer Number (your number in the Vendor's files: have it handy if you call with a query, although Invoices strangely, and infuriatingly, seldom show a telephone number).

An Invoice might look like this (you will have added the freight charge by hand, as it was paid collect):

<table>
<tr><td colspan="2">
WIDGETS INC.
595 Delightful Drive
Slagville NJ 60904
</td><td>
Invoice No. 00654
Date 06/06/97
Your P.O. No. 1835
</td></tr>
<tr><td colspan="2">
Sold to:
ALLGIFTS
The Village
Merchantown, TX 77707
</td><td>
TERMS: Net 30
</td></tr>
<tr><td>9 "Sussex" Cups & Saucers</td><td>@ 7.25</td><td>65.25</td></tr>
<tr><td>7 "Wintergreen" pitchers</td><td>@ 13.50</td><td>94 50</td></tr>
<tr><td colspan="2" align="right">Net Invoice Amount Due</td><td>159.75</td></tr>
<tr><td colspan="2">*Paid Freight Collect Chk #7795*</td><td>11.25</td></tr>
<tr><td colspan="2" align="right">**TDC**</td><td>**171.00**</td></tr>
</table>

If retail is to be at Keystone (100% markup), take TDC × 2 = $342, and divide it by Net Amount Due (the bare cost of the goods): 342 ÷ 159.75 = 2.14

If you have a standard multiplier of, say, 2.25, you now know that using it will make a little extra profit, but if the price looks too high you can reduce it and still make Keystone.

	Arithmetic	Rounded to	Totals
"Sussex"	$7.25 × 2.14 = $15.52.	Say $15.50 ea.	9 × 15.50 = 139.50
	× 2.25 = $16.31.	**Say $16.50 ea.**	**9 × 16.50 = 148.50**
"Wintergreen"	13.50 × 2.14 = $28.89.	Say $28.95 ea.	7 × 28.95 = 202.65
	× 2.25 = $30.38.	**Say $29.95 ea.**	**7 × 29.95 = 209.65**

Yield @ 2.14: $342.15
Yield @ 2.25: $358.15

Having a little in hand enabled us to take the "Wintergreen" to a more saleable price, just below, instead of just over, $30.00

Using 2.14 the Gross Profit is 342.15 – 171.00 = 171.15 = 50.02%
Using 2.25   358.15 – 171.00 = 187.15 = 52.25%

That example shows how you can set your own retails for goods bought at Net, making up for lost profit on goods bought at List less discount, where profit (the discount) will probably be reduced by freight charges, and sometimes also by packing and insurance. If, for instance, you receive $1,000 worth of goods invoiced at List less 50%, but with $13.75 freight, the retail yield will still be the bare $1,000, but the cost of the goods, $500 has been increased to $513.75, leaving only $486.25 profit instead of $500, or 48.6% instead of 50%, a reduction of 1.4%.

A 1.4% reduction in profit may not seem much, but can cause nasty surprises if allowed to happen often, just as a dripping tap can add a surprisingly large amount to your water bill. Accurate costing stops such leaks, by giving you the data for a decision on marking the item higher than the s.r.p., or making up the difference on some other item, as in the Invoice sample above, where the yield is 52.25% using the 2.25 multiplier.

Even though it may not be possible to do much about the Retail of items bought at List, promotions and special deals throughout the year provide ample opportunity to improve Margins on them. Much giftware and dinnerware, for instance, is regularly offered on promotion in both the Spring and the Fall, and there are always promotions of one sort or another for the sales peaks of the year: Valentine's Day, Mother's Day, and on through to Christmas. Orders over a certain size may be shipped freight free, or at a greater discount, or with deferred payment or with some other advantage.

Greater discount on items sold at list will usually be shown as additional to the regular discount. If, for instance, the regular discount is 50% off List, the offer will not be 60%, but will be "50 & 20," *i.e.* for an item at $100 List, there would be 20% off the regular discounted cost of $50, for a net cost of $40 – the same as 60% off List. Such deals give you the option of passing the savings on to your customers (with appropriate advertising) and keeping the regular 50% margin, or maintaining the regular retail, and reaping extra profit.

Costing, in short, depends on three factors: *constant vigilance* to ensure that freight costs do not erode profit on goods invoiced at list; *accurate determination of TDC* when costing goods invoiced at net; and *sound decisions on the amount of markup*, based on the target percentage for cost of goods sold.

Some Costing Hints and Shortcuts (*see also* charts in the Appendix, starting on p. 191.)

As shown in the Invoice for "Sussex" and "Wintergreen" above, to cost a random assortment of items invoiced at net, take the total amount due for the whole Invoice (after adding freight if it has been paid separately), double it, and divide the result by the net cost of the goods alone. In the sample Invoice this came to 2.14, and multiplying the net cost of each item by 2.14 gave Retail at Keystone.

For merchandise bought by the case, retail price per item can be found in one step, as a percentage of the case cost.

For instance, if you buy widgets in cases of a dozen, at $60 the case, and you want 40% margin, retail per widget will be 13.9% of $60, which is $8.34.

The 13.9% was found by assuming that the retail yield of any case of 12 would be $100, making the retail price per item 100 ÷ 12, or $8.33. For 40% margin, the case cost would have to be $60, and 8.33 is 13.9% of 60.

Thus the retail price of any item, packed 12 to the case, and to yield 40% margin, will be 13.9% of case cost whatever that cost may be.

Similarly, for a case of 24, at 30% margin, retail will be $100.00 ÷ 24 = $4.17, which is 5.96% of the $70 case cost, so if you buy a case of 24, and want 30% margin, the retail each will be 5.96% of whatever the case cost may be.

In summary: whatever the quantity per case and the desired margin, assume a case retail yield of $100, and a cost to reflect the desired margin. Divide 100 by the case quantity, and express the result as a percentage of the case cost, which will give retail each.

Always calculate retail price from TDC, not from net cost.

If the retail price comes out higher or lower than you think suitable for the particular item, it will have to be adjusted, but it is essential to adjust from the correct basis, so that the amount of deviation from the budgeted margin is known, and can be compensated for elsewhere.

COST OF GOODS SOLD: Every single expenditure incurred in running the business, plus the Net Income (*if any!*), come out of Gross Profit – what is left after paying for what has been sold. The Cost of Goods Sold (so listed in the Net Income Statement), is therefore the most critical figure in all your accounts after Sales (Expenses – *which see* – are important too, but a 1% change in those will affect Net Income far less than a 1% change in Cost of Goods Sold).
Caution: Net Income is net *operating* income. Capital expenditures, such as for a display unit or a new cash register, are not Expenses. Gross Profit does, of course, finally pay for everything, but only day to day operating expenses are deducted on the Net Income Statement, which is a performance report card, and does not refer to money in the bank (but if you don't make enough Net Income, you will not be able to afford any capital expenditure). *See* Phantom Profit.

Cost of Goods Sold is Opening (start-of-period) Inventory, plus purchases during the period, less Closing (end-of-period) Inventory. It is best monitored as a percentage of Sales, *and the dollar amount of that percentage, other things being equal, goes straight down to the bottom line,* for instance:

An increase of 1% on $500,000 Sales reduces Net Income by $5,000.

The following two scenarios, for an imaginary year, in which Opening Inventory was $125,000, and Expenses $225,000, show how a variation in Closing Inventory can affect Cost of Goods Sold, *and thus the bottom line.*

Scenario 1

A	Gross Sales			500,000
	Opening Inventory	125,000		
	Plus Purchases	275,000		
	Less Closing Inventory	125,000		
B	Cost of Goods Sold	275,000	55.0%	275,000
	GROSS PROFIT (A–B)		45.0%	225,000
	Less Expenses			225,000
	NET INCOME (Loss)		0.0%	0

Scenario 2

A	Gross Sales			500,000
	Opening Inventory	125,000		
	Plus Purchases	275,000		
	Total	400,000		
	Less Closing Inventory	120,000		
B	Cost of Goods Sold	280,000	56.0%	280,000
	GROSS PROFIT (A–B)	220,000	44.0%	220,000
	Less Expenses			225,000
	NET INCOME (Loss)		–1.0%	(5,000)

Cost of Goods Sold is 1% higher, and Net Income is correspondingly decreased. (Closing Inventory was down but Sales stayed flat – more items were sold for the same amount of money).

COUPON. It is always difficult to measure response to advertising. In a mature business, graphs showing past relationships between advertising expenditure and sales, backed up by files of the actual ads, will be very informative; but in a new and growing business, how much growth can be attributed simply to newness, and how much to your advertising? The addition of a coupon to an advertisement, if it is appropriate to your type of business, is one of the surest ways of quantifying response. The range of incentives is limited only by your resources and imagination. but be careful not to infringe any gambling or lottery laws.

A word of warning if you are judging past years: advertising is not the only influence on sales. The most effective or poor advertisement may have coincided with a hurricane or a blizzard (or with a surge of sales-boosting traffic due to some external event), so be sure to consult the Store Diary, as well as the actual advertising records, when judging past performance. (*See also* Advertising).

CREDIT. If Sales are the lifeblood of your business, then good credit with your vendors is the heart that keeps that lifeblood flowing full and strong. Without good credit the flow of merchandise into the store will be slow, insufficient and erratic, and sales will become anemic. With good credit, merchandise will arrive promptly, plentifully and regularly, and Sales will respond accordingly.

Good credit also provides a hidden reservoir of working capital. As pointed out in cash flow, your customers pay cash on the barrel-head, while you buy the merchandise on thirty days' credit. You lose this nice financial cushion if your credit goes bad, and you find yourself paying c.o.d., or, even worse, C.W.O. – cash with order.

C.O.D. is doubly infuriating, as carriers may charge an extra fee for it, but at least you have the goods in hand the moment you pay for them. C.W.O., on the other hand, actually reduces working capital, because, although it may earn a little mitigating extra discount, you will part with your money long before you get the goods; and even then it is not uncommon to find that less has been shipped than you paid for.

If you are opening a new account, most vendors will ask for a bank reference, with the name of your loan officer, and three trade references. However tight the cash flow, it should always be possible to maintain three accounts in good standing so that you can supply references on demand. Without them, you may have to do without a wonderful new line of merchandise because you do not have the cash for C.W.O. or C.O.D. Some vendors are more easy going than others when it comes to references, and some can be very demanding, even asking for your last Financial Statement. This is none of their business, and I have never known a new order turned down for lack of one.

You may encounter a surprising situation if your business structure changes, say from proprietorship to corporation. Some vendors with whom you have been trading on good terms for years may ask for a new set of credit references, because, technically speaking, they are dealing with a new customer – the corporation.

For the most part sales representatives are not concerned with your credit status: it depends on the company. Sometimes head office will ask the sales person to make tactful mention that there is a payment overdue, and at the other extreme, after placing an order with a perfectly friendly sales person, you may get a rude letter from the credit manager, demanding payment for all outstanding invoices before he will clear the order for shipment.

The best way to maintain a good credit rating is to pay all invoices on time, but if that becomes difficult, maintain contact with the credit manager, and "show willing." Except for a very few companies who seem eager to cut off their noses to spite their faces, credit managers generally would rather keep a customer than lose one, but remember: Hell hath no fury like a credit manager ignored.

One excellent way to protect your credit rating is to attend trade shows regularly and get to know the principals of the various companies you deal with. If problems do arise, and you have established good relationships, a personal telephone call can work wonders.

CREDIT CARDS. The business of the shopkeeper is to please the customer, so it pays to accept even the less common cards, although they may yield only one or two sales a week. The customer who is told that you do not accept her card may not make a fuss or stalk out in a fury, but on the other hand she may never come back – and you will never know. Other things being equal, customers will use whichever store makes shopping (and paying) easiest, and if you are that store you have a competitive advantage.

Some stores refuse to accept Credit Card charges below a certain minimum, perhaps $5 or $10. Eagle-eyed bean-counters may be able to prove that it is uneconomical to process such small sums, but the more likely reason is simply that it is "too much trouble." The answer is threefold: first, electronic processing of credit cards is now so quick and easy that the "trouble" is minimal, secondly, the higher the volume on your credit cards, the lower the discount, and thirdly, nothing is too much trouble if it secures a sale and keeps the customer happy. Display signs showing all the cards which you accept, not only by the cash register, but also by the front door, and around the store. Many people dislike asking questions in stores; some will simply leave without buying anything if they do not see the sign for their card. Once again, you may have lost a sale, but you will never know.

The percentage taken by the credit card company can vary considerably, depending on the volume of your business with that particular card, and on how and where you deposit the proceeds. Your choice will depend upon the speed with which the proceeds are available to you, the amount of discount, and the convenience, or otherwise, of processing. Electronic processing not only credits your account immediately, sale by sale or in daily batches, but has the added advantage that it is very easy and convenient for the cashier, who no longer has to use an imprinter, write out a sales slip, or call in for authorization. Offers of very low discounts if you deposit in a particular bank need to be studied with care to make sure that the saving is not canceled out by a transaction or authorization fee charged automatically to every sale.

Credit Card discounts take a significant lump out of Gross Sales, and it is important that they be listed as a separate Expense on the Income Statement, and expressed, like all other items, as a percentage of Gross Sales. Apart from the vital function of showing where the money goes, this also helps in planning, as the rate of credit card use is a clue to the health of the local economy.

There should be individual bookkeeping accounts for each card, as the card company will send a monthly statement, which will need to be reconciled. That statement will also show average transaction amount, and it is important to check this, as the higher it is (provided total sales keep pace) the lower the discount rate, but you may not get a lower rate unless you ask for it. Knowledge of comparative discount rates is also important for the cashier, so that if a customer offers a choice of cards, the one with the lowest rate can be chosen.

CREDIT MEMO FOR RETURNS FROM CUSTOMERS. This is sometimes called a "Due Bill," and is always preferable to cash, except on the rare occasions when it is necessary to give cash just to get a really obstreperous customer out of the store. It is essential to enforce, so far as is humanly possible, the rule that no credit memo can be issued unless the customer has the receipt.

If you do gift wrapping, it is prudent to have a printed label to stick inside the lid of the box, showing the date, the contents, and the names of the donor and the recipient, so that if the recipient wants to return the gift, there is positive identification.

The cashier must be thoroughly trained in handling returns, and there should be a clear notice about them by the cash register (*see also*

Cashier). The morning Cockpit Check (pens, full stapler, spare register tape etc. at the register) will ensure that there are always Credit Memo forms handy, with the store's name and address either printed or rubber stamped.

CREDIT MEMO FROM VENDORS: Vendors may compensate for damage or shortage in a shipment by free replacement or by Credit Memo, which follows exactly the same bookkeeping route as the Invoice. Do not adjust the invoice in response to telephoned assurance that credit is coming: note on it that credit is due, and wait for the actual memo.

CUSTOMERS: How your customers are greeted and treated will to a very large extent determine the character and success of your store. At one extreme you may simply ignore them until they are ready to pay and go. At the other, you greet them effusively when they come in, and stick to them like a limpet all round the store, either trying to sell them things they don't want, or furtively stalking them as suspected shoplifters. Both techniques are equally effective in discouraging a return visit.

The most courteous, and therefore the most effective, way to treat customers is to greet them when they come in, and ask if you can help them find anything, or, if they are already shopping, ask if they are finding what they want. Further contact will depend on the response. The familiar "can I help you?" nowadays often seems to be understood as "Are you ready to pay?" (with "if not, why not?" implied), and can produce a resentful "Not yet" or an icy "Just looking."

There is an old army saying that there are no bad regiments, only bad officers. It could equally be said that in retailing there are no bad customers, only bad shopkeepers. Some customers can indeed be just plain nasty (as can we all, from time to time), and all you can do is treat them as gently as possible. Ninety-nine percent of the time you will find that the soft answer turneth away wrath, and if you address the problem, rather than the emotion, you will not only soothe anger, but may make a friend.

Do not be deceived, either, by first appearances. In my early retailing days, my heart quailed when the door opened to admit a short elderly woman approximately the shape of a mail-box, and with the expression of a bad-tempered frog. She turned out to be a person of enormous intelligence and charm, with a memorably delightful smile, and we all enjoyed her visits for many years.

To enjoy retailing you must enjoy people. They are your business.

D

DAILY DUTIES (If you delegate any, be specific about which, and to whom.)

Before the store opens it is convenient to get some things done:

- ☐ If you did not do it yesterday, this is a good time to open the mail.
- ☐ Check the Answering and Fax Machines.
- ☐ Check all light bulbs.
- ☐ Empty trash cans.
- ☐ Adjust the thermostat to day setting: money is wasted on over-cooling and overheating by those too busy to notice.
- ☐ Go through the Cockpit Check: floor swept, displays checked, refreshed and dusted, everything to hand at the Cash Register.
- ☐ Adjust the sound system: music in the milking shed increases milk yield: music in the showroom raises money yield.
- ☐ Check the calendar for appointments and tax return and advertising deadlines.
- ☐ Check Accounts Payable for Invoices due.

During the day:

- ☐ Attend to customers
- ☐ Pay Invoices and any other payments due.
- ☐ Clean the back room (not called stock-room – there should be no inventory in here)
- ☐ If there is some inventory overflow in the back room, make daily efforts to get it out.
- ☐ Check the Hold and Special Order shelves, to ensure that all merchandise is labeled and current.
- ☐ Check Special Orders and Call Cards, and include them in the Purchase Orders below.
- ☐ Write replenishment Purchase Orders.
- ☐ Write new merchandise Purchase Orders.

- ☐ Check in, price, and put on display any new deliveries, not forgetting to put aside and label any Special Order and Call Card items.
- ☐ Check the stock in the store cupboard: toilet paper, paper towels, Windex, pricing gun labels, receipt and calculator tapes, merchandise bags, etc.
- ☐ *Inspect the whole store as if you are a customer, starting outside with the window displays.* You are managing a whole forest, not just attending to individual trees.

At closing:

- ☐ Reconcile the Cash Register.
- ☐ Make the Bank Deposit.
- ☐ Adjust the thermostat to night setting.
- ☐ Close down and turn off computers, if you have them.
- ☐ Turn out the lights.
- ☐ Lock the doors (yes, police have found open doors, and called forgetful owners in the middle of the night).
- ☐ Put the Bank Deposit in the night drop on the way home.

See Time Management.

DATING: Vendors will occasionally offer a "dating program," particularly in connection with a special seasonal sales effort. Details may vary from a simple extension of credit to sixty days from the normal thirty, provided a minimum order is placed, up to a staggered payment plan covering several months, for very large orders. An example of the latter might be a Christmas program, with a minimum order of $20,000 to be placed by May 30th, for delivery 1st September, 10% payable 1st November, 40% 1st December, and 50% 1st January.

There are many variations, but they all offer the undoubted advantage of giving you more time to sell the goods before having to pay for them. If you have reasonable confidence in your sales projections, are not tempted into over-ordering, and have your cash flow planned to meet the payment schedule, dating programs are well worth-while, particularly when they include, as they sometimes do, a little extra discount.

Other programs may also offer extra discount for large orders placed early, but with no extension of normal credit. These swell inventory above regular levels, so you must either pass the discount on in hopes of faster sales, or maintain the regular retail price in hopes that the extra profit will compensate for the longer return on your money.

DEADLINES: Federal, state, county, city & school district authorities all want some of your money, and impose penalties if they do not get it on time. The full federal list is available from the IRS, *Publication 509*, but state and local requirements will, of course, vary. Your CPA can be of the greatest help in the accurate and timely filing of all returns.

A suggested chart of deadlines is given in the Appendix, p. 188.

DEBIT and CREDIT: *see* Double Entry Bookkeeping.

DECISION MAKING: Never rely on instinct.

One of the first lessons for pilots learning to fly on instruments is that the instruments do not lie, instinct does. You may be convinced that you are climbing, while the instruments say that you are going down: trust the instruments.

In retailing, you may be convinced that a certain item is selling well, because you happen to have been in the showroom and seen a couple of sales. Check your instruments – quantity of original order, date, quantity remaining – before reordering.

Again, a run of good sales days may inspire you to make a big capital purchase or undertake some other expensive project. Do not do it until you have checked current Net Income, the Cash Flow Forecast, and the Budget. It is only too easy to feel that you are climbing, when in fact the figures show the opposite.

Take heart, however, for the reverse is also true. It is only too easy for the single-handed overworked owner, after a few dull days and some difficult customers, to feel that all is lost and that the business is going down. A good look at the figures will probably show that his fears are unfounded, and that the business is climbing nicely.

Every decision in retailing is ultimately financial, and no decision should ever be made without checking the financial instruments. It is a truism that most business failures are due to bad record keeping, and the reason is obvious: without good records, decisions have to be made on instinct.

DELEGATING AUTHORITY: You may be an absentee owner who delegates full authority to a manager, or an owner-operator who delegates selected in-store tasks such as bookkeeping or display. Whatever the level of delegation, you must retain ultimate control, make clear the results you want, and specify the scope and limits of the job. Simply leaving a job to an employee without these safeguards is to abdicate responsibility rather than to delegate authority, and may produce results you do not want and which may be difficult to correct.

DELIVERY: Ordering is only half the battle. Getting the merchandise delivered on time, undamaged, at minimum cost, is the other half. Modern packing techniques and materials have reduced breakage and damage to a fraction of delivered values and quantities, and that is dealt with under claims. Also there may be delay if your account is overdue, and this is discussed under credit.

There remain three other factors: cost, speed, accuracy.

Cost

1. Many vendors deliver "Fgt. pd." for orders over a stated minimum value. This is usually low enough to be met without overloading inventory, but a balance must be struck between the savings on the freight, and the rate of sale. A few vendors set minimums by weight, and will pay freight on an order over, say, 500 lb., which is the minimum set by the freight company, who will accept less, but still charge for 500 lb.

2. Vendors' minimums should apply to the amount ordered, not the amount shipped. Intentional exceptions to this are very rare, but it pays to check when ordering, and also when receiving, to make sure that you do not carelessly pay freight on what should have been a free shipment. It is also necessary to check that back orders from a fgt. pd. shipment are also fgt. pd., even though the back-order shipment itself may be well under minimum.

3. A "Freight Allowance" is often available. It may be for the total freight or for only half, but in either case it means that you pay the freight, but can deduct the amount from the invoice if it is paid on time. If it is paid late, the amount is disallowed.

4. Choice of shipper is usually up to the vendors, who will ship by whatever freight company gives the best value in terms of cost,

breakage and reliability. If you feel you can get a better deal, you may, of course, specify a shipper.

Speed

1. If delivery time is critical, and you call the order in by phone, make sure that everything you order is in stock. An assurance that "all orders are shipped within 24 hours" means only that what is in stock will be shipped, not that your order will be complete. Follow up with written confirmation (but with "Confirmation – do not duplicate" writ large across it), and if you fax the order, ask for confirmation from their end.

2. Do not be content with "we'll get that out today": this sometimes means only that the paper work will be done today, and it will take several more days actually to get the order on the truck.

3. For emergency shipments, do not hesitate to sacrifice profit to speed. Use UPS Overnight, or Second Day Air, or Federal Express, or whatever such service may be available.

Accuracy

1. Inaccuracies in individual shipments are mostly minor, but left uncorrected can cause real problems in inventory control and maintenance of profit margins.

2. Check in all merchandise carefully against the Packing List, the Purchase Order, and the Invoice. The Packing List lists what is in the shipment, but often shows no prices. It must be checked against the Invoice to see that what has been sent is exactly what has been charged, and the Invoice in turn must be checked against the Purchase Order to see that what has been charged is exactly what was ordered and, most important, that the prices charged are as ordered.

3. **Never assume that the price is the same as last time.** Terms are nearly always "prices ruling at time of delivery," and "prices may be changed without notice," so what the sales rep told you when you placed the order may have been true then, but altered since.

Typical problems:

- Contents of carton mis-described on Packing List.
- Items in carton not on Packing List, and vice versa.
- Packing List and/or actual items do not match Invoice.

- Packing List and/or actual items do not match Purchase Order.
- Goods charged on Invoice not as ordered.
- Substitute items shipped and charged when "No Substitutes" was specified on Purchase Order.

Vendors are usually very willing to correct mistakes, because they cause as much trouble to them as they do to you, and it is here that a good sales representative can be helpful, by coming in and seeing the problem on the spot, and reporting to head office that it is genuine.

DEPARTMENTS: Sales must be analyzed by category as well as by item, and although a small store will not have departments in the same sense as a Department Store, it is helpful, when classifying the inventory, to think in terms of Departments rather than categories.

This forces you to look at the inventory from the customer's point of view, using her perception of what goes with which, to ensure that all items in one category – one Department – exert that mutual sales leverage over each other which is such a strong stimulant to sales.

Particularly in a small store, this will help with display, as the inventory print-out from the office, if arranged by Departments, will be a guide to what is available and what belongs where, and the daily sales analysis from the cash register can be coded to match.

This is essentially a matter of thinking like a shopkeeper, not a bureaucrat. A bureaucrat would put leather billfolds and leather women's purses under "Leather," while a shopkeeper will put the billfolds into Men's Gifts department, and the purses into Ladies' Accessories Department.

Thinking by Department also helps decisions in Purchasing. When looking at a new product, it is essential to consider how it will fit in with the other merchandise, and in which department. If it does not seem to fit anywhere, it must either be rejected, or the plunge must be taken to create a new Department – but that will involve finding other, complementary, merchandise, and a whole new investment. However tempting a new line may seem, it must either fit into the existing Department structure, or be strong enough to anchor a new department of its own, but the new department itself must fit into the rest of the store. The new merchandise must be, even in the most general terms, the sort of thing which your customers expect to find in your sort of store. A very successful gift shop once brought in an excellent line of casual beachwear. Design, quality and price were right on the mark, but the line was a total failure: it was in the wrong store.

DEPRECIATION: Although this will appear on the Income Statement as an Expense, it is not a cash outlay, so it is tempting to dismiss it as a technical entry put in by your CPA, without immediate relevance. This is a mistake.

In manufacturing, the critical importance of depreciation is obvious. Machinery wears out and becomes obsolete, and if funds are not available to replace it there will be no product to sell. In retailing, the actual existence of the merchandise does not depend on depreciable equipment such as the copy machine, the computer, and the display units, or on the physical state of the premises, but if these deteriorate and are not replaced, office work becomes less efficient, the store attracts fewer customers, and the business goes downhill. Even if they far outlive their legally depreciable life, their capital cost must be recovered, so that they can be replaced when the time does come.

It is important, therefore, to look at Depreciation from two angles. First, the dollar amount shown in the Net Income Statement: this is indeed a technical entry, and is an annual fraction of the purchase price of each item, the amount depending on the number of years of useful life allotted to it by the IRS. If, for instance, the rules say that you may depreciate a computer over five years, in the sixth year after purchase there would be no further depreciation shown for it in the accounts.

The two examples below show the difference depreciation can make in a Net Income Statement

This example *omits* it:

SALES	100,000
Cost of Goods Sold	<u>50,000</u>
GROSS PROFIT	50,000
Expenses	<u>47,500</u>
Depreciation	—
NET INCOME	**<u>$2,500</u>**

This example *includes* it:

SALES	100,000
Cost of Goods Sold	50,000
GROSS PROFIT	50,000
Expenses	47,500
Depreciation	3,000
NET LOSS	**($500)**

The first example shows a nice cash Net Income of $2,500, but it does not allow for the fact that cash may be needed to replace, perhaps, a computer and a copy machine, and that the capital outlay on some Leasehold Improvements needs to be recovered.

The second example shows the danger of this omission. The business is not actually making enough to cover its future needs. If the situation is not rectified, it will manage for a while on its deceptive cash income, but eventually it will feel the deadly effects of ignoring Depreciation.

To calculate a true figure for Depreciation, your CPA must know the items concerned, the initial cost of each and the dates of purchase. Keep a register, including details of method of payment. This will also assist in annual inventory: your CPA may, for instance, show a desk on the books which in fact you sold during the year without telling him. Taking annual inventory of such assets at the same time as regular merchandise inventory is the only way to ensure that the Accounts give a true picture (take inventory also of small non-depreciable items such as staplers: Office Supplies can add up to a surprisingly large Expense, which needs to be tightly controlled).

No mention has been made of the effect of Depreciation on Taxes (although it is certainly a deductible Expense), nor have I given a table of depreciation rates or any list of depreciable assets. My purpose throughout this book is to demonstrate how Bookkeeping and Accounting can and should be used to help you make decisions in everyday operational management: your CPA will explain how to calculate depreciation, and what is depreciable over what periods, and he or she will furthermore be completely up to date, which no book such as this can be.

DETAILS: Trivial flaws will not destroy your advertising or your Image, and the customer may not even notice them, but they can put the message just a tiny bit out of focus. The Lincoln Continental, for instance, calls itself, on the back, a Continental Lincoln, and when you squeeze Crest toothpaste from your left hand, the name is upside down. Do these trivia matter? No, no more than a dirty TV screen, but it is worth a little extra trouble to make sure that your store's image is always in clear sharp focus.

DIARY: Keep a Store Diary. It will compel you to consider each day's business in an orderly and disciplined manner, and it will also show you comparisons with previous years, revealing the continuing influences of time and events upon your business, and giving you a deeper understanding of how it works.

A Diary is also a great help in minor decisions, such as whether to close or stay open on some State or Federal holidays when there is no uniformity among neighborhood stores, as it will tell you what you did last year (it's surprisingly easy to forget), and whether you regretted closing because all neighboring stores were open and busy, or whether, if you were open, it was worth it. It should also tell you who worked that day, which will make staffing decisions easier this year.

Gross Sales in the sample Diary page below can be simply the Bank Deposit less non-sales income. This gives a rough-and-ready figure, not adjusted for returns, or lay-away payments or suchlike, but is good enough if you do not have the true Net Sales figure, as the importance of the Diary is not the actual dollar amount, but the day-to-day comparison with last year on the same basis, with Hours of Business/Sales per Hour, Weather, Advertising, Holidays and other influential events factored in. This is something the Accounts cannot do.

The Diary should be in Page-a-Day form, showing Date, Day of the Week (noting special days, such as Father's Day etc.), the financial comparisons, Hours Open and Sales per Hour (Sales figures will be very misleading if you are open regular hours this year, but do not remember that last year you stayed open late), Weather (a blizzard last year will explain a 100% increase this year, and vice versa), Staff on duty, Advertisements running, and lastly Remarks, which will record such events as remodeling, renewal of the lease, demonstration by a manufacturer's visiting artist, or anything else in the store or the neighborhood which has affected the day's sales.

SHOP DIARY.

Day: ___________________ **Date:** ___________________________

Holiday (if any) ____

Today's Bank Deposit $ ____________

Less non-sales income
   (*e.g.* **Insurance claim check**) $

Today's Gross Sales $ ____________

Same day of the week (*not date*)
   last year Gross Sales $ ____________

Difference, dollars $ ____________

Difference, percent   ____________ %

Year-to-Date Gross Sales $ ____________

Last Year-to-Date Gross Sales $ ____________

Difference, dollars $ ____________

Difference, percent   ____________ %

Number of hours open   ____________

Gross Sales per Hour   **This Year** $ ____________

                                Last Year $ ____________

                                Difference $ ____________

                                Difference % ____________

Staff on duty ____

____

Weather ____

Advertisements running _________________________________

Remarks ____

____

A Diary is useful if you are running the store yourself, but indispensable if you are much away, or employ a manager.

The layout opposite may not exactly suit you, and it can conveniently be combined with the Daily Cash Form described under Reconciling the Register, but do at least show some year-to-year comparisons, and explain differences. Remember that those who ignore history are condemned to repeat it.

DISCOUNTS. One of the first rules of business is "take your discounts." Under "Terms" on the invoice you may see "2/10 Net 30," meaning that you may deduct 2% if you pay within 10 days, or pay the full amount within the usual thirty.

Taking the discount makes an immediate contribution to Gross Profit, by reducing cost of goods sold, and, as pointed out under costing, any reduction in Cost of Goods Sold goes straight to the bottom line. Taking two percent on an invoice for perhaps as little as $25 may not seem important, but it is part of the essential discipline of stripping every invoice down to its bare-bones net cost. No invoice should be paid unless it has been picked clean as a skeleton. Anything left on the bones reduces your profit.

If you do miss discounts, they are deductible as an Expense, "Discounts Missed," but it is obviously best to keep up-to-date and take the discounts.

DISPLAY: No activity in retailing is so challenging as the creation and maintenance of effective display: I almost said attractive and effective, but some displays can be very effective without being, except in the most literal sense, attractive. An effective display is one that sells merchandise: if it does, it is good display: if it does not, then however beautiful and imaginative it is, it is bad display. The style of your displays will depend both upon the overall character of your store, and on the nature of the merchandise, but in any case you will probably have three categories: general merchandise on shelves, tables, and display units; special feature displays calling attention to new merchandise or seasonal attractions; and last but by no means least, the store windows. Impressive careers have been devoted entirely to the art of display, so I will confine myself here to a few very basic suggestions:

- Look at every move you make from the customer's point of view.

- Do not use merchandise to create effects which do not emphasize the merchandise itself.

- Ideally, all merchandise, unless in special displays such as table settings, should be at, or a little below, eye level. As this is impractical, you have to concentrate the more important pieces as near to this ideal as possible, with others above and below, but not higher than can be comfortably reached by little old ladies, and not lower than knee-level.

- You may certainly display merchandise to advantage above and below these limits, but it should duplicate what is on the selling levels.

- Do not make special displays into such works of art that customers either are afraid to touch them, or will wreck them if they do. Create some wonderfully elaborate center-piece, perhaps, to attract attention, but make sure that the merchandise around it is easily accessible by the customer, and easily rearranged after it has been picked over.

- For general stock items commonsense is the rule. Tall items at the back and short in front – all variations of the same design in the same place (how many sales have been lost because the customer saw the pink, but wanted the blue, which she never saw because it was displayed separately?); every piece easily reached; clear prices; good lighting.

- As to lighting: a halogen spotlight will make merchandise jump out of its background like a jack-in-the-box, but the effect will be wasted if the heat fries the customers head. As always, stand where the customer will stand and ask yourself "Am I tempted? If not, why not?"

- Goods must be clearly, fully, and neatly labeled. For every customer who asks a question, is answered, and buys, there are untold legions who wonder, say nothing, and depart. None of us will ever know how many sales have been lost because of bad labeling, but we can rest assured there will be none if the customer can find out all she wants without having to ask.

- Window display is only useful if it interests the public outside, and if there is a public outside to be interested. If your store is in a location which enjoys much foot traffic, then you need window display. Similarly, if your store is in a strip shopping center, you need window display that will attract the attention of motorists looking for some other store. Before you even start considering what to put in the window, however, you must establish the window's role in relation to the interior of the store.

You may want to treat the windows simply as showcases for the street with their blind backs to the showroom. This, of course, means that the merchandise is difficult to get at, and must be duplicated inside. It also requires considerable skill at "window dressing," to attract attention and pull people into the store, but at the same time it provides the greatest possible scope for creative and imaginative effects. Disadvantages of the "showcase" window are that it blocks out the light, and prevents people from seeing into the store.

A shelf or platform level with the window-sill, and bearing merchandise angled to the window-shopper, is both effective and easy to maintain (provided it is not too wide). It also allows the window to fulfill its original function of lighting the interior, and gives the passing shopper a view of the whole store, not just a few selected pieces. With careful arrangement, the display can be as effective for the customer inside, so you are not sacrificing any in-store display space. Make sure that the lighting illuminates the merchandise for the window shoppers outside, without dazzling the customers inside. It needs to be on the wall above the window, and shining almost straight down.

A glass display unit right up against the window can be very effective. Again, merchandise is visible from outside and accessible from inside, while window-shoppers can still see right past the merchandise into the body of the store.

The only "wrong" type of window display is one that is dirty, untidy or permanent. A clean, well-maintained and fresh display (however unconventional) is a good display if it brings in customers. In this connection, beware of the damaging effects of sunlight and heat on the merchandise. Particularly in the hotter parts of the country it is virtually impossible to display books, foods, textiles, or anything packaged in printed paper or cardboard in a south-facing window for more than a day or two without fading or other damage. Tinted glass is a help, but it so reduces visibility from outside (and dulls the colors of the goods) that it is hardly worth bothering with a window display at all. In a mall, of course, the problem does not arise.

DISPLAY UNITS: Selection of display units will depend on the type of store and the merchandise, but there will always be a choice between new and used, custom built or off the shelf, free-standing or built-in, and some owners may enjoy making their own.

Some manufacturers, too, will supply special units for their own merchandise. These are usually available either as a straight purchase, or on favorable terms with a sufficiently large order. Some such units are carefully designed and ideal for the purpose, and well worth having if the price is right, and if there is room for them. Others, however, are just standard products with the vendor's name on, and may or may not be worthwhile.

When selecting or designing a unit, be very clear as to its purpose. There is nothing worse than finding that the unit which looked so wonderful on the drawing board or in the showroom is, in fact, quite unsuitable for any of your merchandise.

Custom-built units are expensive, but have the great advantage that you get exactly what you want. Deciding and defining what you want, however, is not easy, and part of the expense will be the fees of a professional store designer. Also custom-built fittings rely on a very specific vision of future trading, which can limit your freedom to adapt if projections are wrong or market conditions change.

Used display units are often as good as new, but the temptation to get something which is not quite what you need, just because it is cheap, can cause much subsequent regret.

Lighted units are extremely effective, but before buying consider the power supply. This will probably present no problem if the unit backs onto a wall, but if it is free-standing getting a cord to it may be difficult.

Lastly, be sure that all units are of manageable size, and reasonably mobile. It can be very limiting and frustrating to have a unit which requires four strong men to move it, and all units should either be on casters, or at least glides. It is extremely important to be able to change the store around without having to call in the Seabees. *See also* Furniture, Fixtures and Fittings, Tools *and* Equipment *and* Some Assembly Required.

DISTRIBUTOR: Merchandise is sometimes available from a Distributor as well as direct from the Importer or Manufacturer. Direct order has the advantage of lower price but this may be offset by an uncomfortably large minimum order requirement, and by freight charges, whereas buying from a Distributor has the advantage that you can place much smaller orders (probably with less freight and quicker delivery if there are regional warehouses) but the price will be higher. The decision can only be made on a case-by-case basis, depending on how fast the item sells, its Profit Margin, and the freight charges. One major advantage of distributors, which should never be forgotten, is that they often have stock when the actual Manufacturer or Importer does not, which can be very useful if you have impatient customers, or if there is a block in the regular flow of important items which you normally get direct.

In some trades, hardware for instance, distributors are the rule rather than the exception, and it may not be possible to order some products directly from manufacturers.

DOGS: Faithful hounds waiting patiently outside the store are more than welcome, and giving a thirsty beast a bowl of water on a hot day is not only kind, but good public relations. They should not, however, be allowed inside. City ordnance probably prohibits them anyway, and most certainly does if you carry any foods. Some people, unfortunately, carry small dogs everywhere like babes in arms, and you will need both tact and judgment in dealing with them, especially as it can be said, as a general rule, that the smaller the dog, the richer the customer.

DONATIONS. *See* Charity.

DOUBLE ENTRY BOOKKEEPING: It is not the purpose of this book to teach bookkeeping, but to demonstrate its importance in management. However, to make best use of it one must understand the fundamental principle that every Debit is balanced by a Credit, and vice versa. There is an example under Petty Cash of how this works, with an explanation of the apparent contradiction that when you write a check, for instance, it is recorded in the Checking Account as a Credit.

Beware of confusion if you use off-the-shelf software. Basic bookkeeping stationery has two columns; Debit, and Credit, in that order. A bookkeeper writing in a ledger would therefore enter a check drawn on the account in the second column – Credit. In at least one program, however, Quickbooks™, the check register is designed to make things easier for the amateur, and not only are the columns headed Payments and Deposits instead of Debit and Credit, but they are in that reverse order, so that anyone who has learned standard bookkeeping will be confused by having to enter checks in the first column and deposits in the second, exactly opposite to what he or she has been taught.

DROP SHIP. Some vendors will, if asked, ship a special order directly to your customer, and send the invoice to you in the normal way. This is a useful service, but not common, especially among the larger companies. There may also be a small extra charge.

E

EARNED INCOME: income from operations, as opposed to income from sale of an asset, or settlement of an insurance claim, etc.

EFFICIENCY: In a notoriously labor-intensive business like retailing it is imperative, as Kipling put it, to "fill the unforgiving minute with sixty seconds worth of distance run." Productive time, for the specialty retailer, is time spent with customers. All other work is non-productive, and the time spent on it must be cut to a minimum. There are opportunities for time-saving at the cash register, at gift wrapping, at receiving and shipping, in the Office (Planning, Bookkeeping and Administration), and at Housekeeping. Remember at all points that you are running a business, not a household hobby: use commercial or industrial grade equipment.

Here are a few suggestions:

- At the cash register, electronic credit card processing has virtually eliminated hand imprinting, and is now standard equipment. The bar-code reader, discussed more fully under computers, will immensely speed up cash register check-out, and although a little expensive, it will defer or eliminate the need for a second cashier as business increases. Efficiency, however, is in lay-out as well as electronics: assorted sizes of bags must be tidily stored and readily to hand, and there should be a low shelf on which they can be filled. Filling a bag at full counter height, with the top under your chin, is awkward and slow. Similarly, the giftwrap table must be handy, as must the telephone (with message pad), and credit card terminal.

- The giftwrap table must be of sufficient size and comfortable height, with good scissors, bow-making machine, dispensers for tie-cord and fancy ribbons, and for rolls of giftwrap paper (at least two; regular and wedding wrap), scotch tape dispenser, and convenient, well-organized storage for tissue paper and gift boxes. Gift wrapping can be a tiresome and frustrating chore, or, with efficient layout and good equipment, it can be a productive skill to be proud of. The importance of gift wrap is emphasized under that heading.

- Receiving and Shipping of merchandise should be done in the back-room, and they should be physically separate. It is asking for trouble to do both at one table: there is too much chance of delay and error when a large shipment is being checked in, on the same day that an order has to go out to a customer.

- At the Receiving table, there should be a hook for a clipboard holding the Purchase Order, Packing List and, if it has come, the Invoice, so that time is not wasted looking for them after you have put something down on top of them. You will also need a box-cutter (not a little pocket razor-blade holder), a pair of scissors, and a substantial two or three tier four-wheel trolley for the goods as they are unpacked. This keeps the receiving table itself clear, and the trolley can be wheeled straight into the showroom for the goods to be priced (if that wasn't done when they were unpacked) and put on display. To get shipments to the receiving table (and sometimes to help a driver unload) you will also need a two-wheel cart. This should be flat-backed and suitable for cartons large and small: avoid the type which has curved cross-pieces up the back. These are very common and quite unsuitable. Do not get a cart with too long a foot: a short foot will support large cartoons perfectly well when tilted and is much easier to release from under the load.

- For shipping out, there must again be a good table of convenient height, a neatly stored supply of various sizes of carton (saved from incoming merchandise if volume does not justify buying new), an industrial grade hand dispenser for package sealing tape, a heavy scotch tape dispenser, good scissors and a box-cutter (for re-opening parcels when something has been left out, and for tailoring old cartons to new sizes), plus ample supplies of plastic bubble wrap and plastic peanuts (both of which can be saved from incomings). A great convenience and floor-space saver is a large canvas hopper hung from the ceiling (if it is high enough), for the plastic peanuts, which are released by a simple hand-grip from a spout at the bottom. It is hung from a pulley, and can easily be lowered for filling. For shipping, as in receiving, a clipboard hook is needed, so that the all-important customer's enclosure card, cash register receipt, shipping label, etc., do not get lost.

- In the Office, Efficiency depends on the computer, the copy machine, the fax, and, of course, the telephone. These, however, are merely tools, and will not help you to lay your hands on a piece of paper when you want it. Efficiency in the office depends primarily on lay-out and discipline, and the whole point is to ensure that you spend as little time there as possible.

- As to lay-out: in a factory, Efficiency can be measured by widgets per hour, and management will go to great pains to ensure that parts flow to and from the operators smoothly, and that everything they need is in hand's reach, so that they never have to leave their machines. In the office, although you produce no widgets, your desk is your machine, and while using it you should never have to leave it. Plan the office so that incoming and outgoing mail trays are to hand; so that you can reach a Purchase Order form without getting up; so that you only have to swivel in your chair for the fax or the copy machine, so that the telephone is always within reach, and so that you can easily reach the filing cabinet (legal size: letter size is too small for much of what you will receive; and use colored folders: perhaps yellow for catalogs, blue for Purchase Orders, and danger-warning red for Accounts Payable). A good desk and chair are of course essential, but are very personal choices. Beware, however, of computer desks. They look wonderfully efficient, but some appear to be designed for the paperless office. Not everything you do can be computerized, and you will need space for old-fashioned writing, reading, and sorting of documents. Also, bear cost in mind. In the retail business there is nobody to impress with a lavish office except yourself.

- As to Discipline: just as in a factory the finest machine is useless with an untrained, careless or lazy operator, so in the office, you will find the unforgiving minutes flapping round your head like money-vultures if you do not open the mail and deal with it promptly, if you do not keep your filing up-to-date, and if you do not calendar your appointments, your deadlines for advertising, and, most important, for tax-returns.

- Measure your office efficiency by charging yourself an imaginary fee for time spent in the office, fines for missed appointments and deadlines, and penalties for every minute spent searching for un-filled or misplaced documents.

- In Housekeeping, much time can be saved if you have the right equipment (particularly for floor maintenance), and if it is readily to hand. A store cupboard is essential, for paper towels, and Windex, and the many other supplies needed for daily business, such as tapes for the cash register, calculator, and credit card terminal, stationery, paper clips, pens, pencils, business cards, push pins, scotch tape, etc. This not only keeps them handy, but also ensures that you do not waste money buying duplicates because you could not find what you had. If you have bought the right equipment and supplies, and if you never have to waste time looking for them, your Housekeeping will be at maximum efficiency and minimum cost.

EMPLOYEE LEASING. Maintaining Payroll, with accurate deductions, forms and timely tax returns, is tedious and time-consuming. It is only too easy for the uninitiated to make mistakes, and for the busy to miss deadlines, leading to expensive penalties. It is also impossible nowadays for a small business to provide health coverage for its employees.

The solution, for the small business with enough employees (perhaps five, including yourself), is to use Employee Leasing. You and your staff become employees of the leasing company, which leases you back to your business. Your only responsibility is to give the leasing company the hours worked and salaries for each pay period. They will invoice you for the gross amount, plus a small percentage for their fee (which is good value for the time and trouble saved). They, as your employer, handle everything else; all tax returns, W-2s etc. All hiring, firing, and wage-scale decisions remain yours, but you are freed of all the work and responsibility involved in the preparation of payroll and its attendant tax returns, and the administration of retirement plans such as 401(K).

Access to affordable health insurance is a major advantage of Employee Leasing. The leasing company has many small (and large) business clients, and its payroll is consequently that of a very large company, which enables it to offer low group rates. This will mean substantial savings over individual rates which you or your staff may have been paying, and will also enable you to offer health care when hiring, which will strengthen your hand considerably, as virtually no small business can now afford to do so.

Select an employee leasing company with care. The good ones are very good indeed, and offer a wide range of supplementary personnel services which are extremely useful, but there are, as in every business, some companies which are best avoided.

ENTERTAINMENT. There will be occasions when you will have to buy someone a business lunch, but they will be few and far between: the small retailer's expenses for Entertainment should indeed be small. An Entertainment account offers strong temptation, especially if there is a corporate credit card, to stretch the meaning of "business," reducing your profits, and perhaps prompting awkward questions from the IRS if you are audited.

EQUITY and DEBT. A business can be financed with Equity or with Debt, separately or together.

Equity means a share in the business. In a corporation, investors who buy stock acquire Equity. The advantage of financing a business in this way is that you never have to repay the money as a lump sum: you do, however, have to make it earn profits which the investor hopes will repay him many times over. Investments, however, are not loans, and investors accept the risk of losing their money. The disadvantage of this method of financing is that stockholders understandably want a say in how the business is run. (If you are sole proprietor, your original investment and any profits which you leave in the business, will appear in the Accounts as "Owner's Equity").

Debt, on the other hand, has to be repaid within a fixed period, and pay interest. This has the disadvantages of placing you under strict legal obligation, and of giving you use of the money for only a limited time, but has the advantage of leaving you in full control of operations and full ownership of profits (albeit reduced by interest payments).

EROSION. This word is often scorned as a euphemism for shoplifting, which itself should be scorned as a euphemism for theft. It is, however, much more than that, and is a legitimate and useful word describing the reduction of your inventory due to theft by customers (and, alas, employees), and by breakage, damage, shop-soil (made unsaleable by too much handling), and all the other hazards to which retail merchandise is subject.

Unfortunately it is as difficult to keep track of as it is impossible to stop. It can be curbed and limited by ceaseless vigilance and in-store discipline, but in the end there will always be an unhappy gap between what ought to be in stock, and what is actually counted when you take physical inventory.

One of the major advantages of fully computerized Inventory Control (automatic adjustment of Inventory sale by sale, through the cash register) is that it keeps running totals, so that you can compare physical and computer inventory on individual items whenever convenient. This will reveal any Erosion, and if done with some regularity and frequency, will also identify vulnerable areas, and make it easier to take corrective action.

This process, with sources of error being constantly found and corrected, makes the computer figures increasingly reliable as time goes on, but the computer can never completely free the retailer from the annual chore of taking physical inventory.

Erosion

EVENTS. The aim of an Event is obviously to increase sales, but its actual character will depend upon its main purpose, which may be to sell more to existing customers; to attract new customers; to introduce new lines of merchandise, or to enhance the image of the store. Some events will do all these at once, but there is usually a dominant theme.

There is no point in mounting an Event unless you are satisfied that the return will justify the expense. This may not be easy, as some events will not result in immediate extra sales, but in any case keep accurate records of event-related costs (which will be useful if you repeat it), and try to assess results by comparing sales of featured products over a period of time before and afterwards.

The store diary must contain full details of Events, particularly their financial results, because these create anomalies which will need to be explained when the year's month-by-month performance comes up for review. Also, a repeat performance will be much easier if there is a diary record, as will a decision as to whether to repeat at all.

Some suggestions: to sell more to existing customers, you might arrange for a figurine painter from the factory to give a demonstration of her art in the store. The company's sales representative will be able to tell you if such a program is available (if he has not already tried to sell it to you), and what the cost will be (there is usually a requirement for a minimum order value, and for a specific amount of advertising). Timing will be largely out of your control, as it will depend on the demonstrator's schedule. This type of event needs to be very carefully advertised, so that you target customers most likely to be interested, and specifically, if you know them, any collectors. Success here will depend on the depth and accuracy of your Mailing List (this is where a computerized cash register proves its worth, by supplying a list of exactly the right customers).

To introduce a new line of merchandise, much broader advertising will be necessary. Because you will want to attract as many people as possible, both old customers and new, particularly if the new merchandise adds a new dimension to the store. For selected regular customers you might put on a "sneak preview" evening party with refreshments, by invitation, while for the rest, and to attract newcomers, there would be a broadly advertised event during normal business hours the next day.

You or your staff may be qualified to give talks on specific subjects, such as dinnerware, or crystal, or table-settings, and evening events can not only stimulate interest, but also create a loyal following of customers who will depend on you for information and expert advice.

Some manufacturers have videotapes available on loan, and a showing combined with a display of the products makes an excellent event.

These are just a few typical ideas; there are as many more as you can think of.

EXCLUSIVE. There are obvious advantages in being the only store in town to carry a particularly successful line of merchandise, and if you can arrange such a deal you will be very fortunate. Beware, however, of the sales representative who suggests to you that exclusivity will make the item sell. It is the quality of the goods which makes the exclusivity successful, not the exclusivity which makes the goods successful, although you may, of course, back your own judgment on a new and unproved line, and go for exclusivity in the hopes that you have spotted a winner.

On the other side of the exclusive coin is the vendor who says he has exclusive rights to a product, claiming that you can get it from no one else. This may well be true, but should not be taken on trust. Even if the vendor makes his claim in perfect good faith, it does not follow that the manufacturer or importer who has given him the "exclusive" has been strictly honest. The only way to check on this is to know your trade. Keep your eyes open when shopping in your Trade Center, watch your vendors' catalogs, keep a close eye on the trade press, and gossip with your reps.

EXPENSES. Expenses (sometimes called Overhead) are the operating costs which are deducted from Gross Profit to arrive at Net Income. They are repetitive costs, such as rent and utilities; service costs, such as professional fees and payroll; and supply costs such as office supplies, merchandise bags, etc. Advertising, for instance, is an Expense, but the cost of a new computer is not (but its depreciation is). *See also* Financial Statement.

Overhead Expenses

F

F.O.B. (normally seen in lower case – f.o.b.) stands for Free On Board, which originally meant that the manufacturer would pay for delivering the goods as far as the ship. Nowadays, it is still occasionally used to show who will pay any type of freight. If the manufacturer is in Hoboken and your store is in Houston, the invoice might read "f.o.b. Hoboken" meaning you pay the freight, or "f.o.b. Houston" meaning that he does.

FAX. A few years ago fax machines did not exist, then people started asking if you had a fax machine, and now they simply ask for your fax number. We may even have come to the point where to say that you do not have a Fax number is to convey the unfortunate impression that you cannot afford it. Even if that is true, however, you should get one as soon as possible, because many people will want to send you a Fax rather than telephone or write, and you yourself will indeed soon find it indispensable. It is much easier – and quicker – to put a Purchase Order in the fax machine and press a button than it is to put it in an envelope, stick on a stamp, and get it in the mail. Also, if you fax a document, you still have it, and there is no need to make a file copy.

FINANCIAL STATEMENT: The full Financial Statement for a business is more elaborate than the single-sheet versions which most of us have completed for private loans of one sort and another. It will certainly contain the Balance Sheet and the Net Income Statement, plus supporting documents such as a Statement of Retained Earnings, Statement of cash flow, and Changes in Equity. It will come with a covering letter from the CPA, and will incorporate his (or her) Notes on the Accounts.

For management purposes, the two vital documents are the Balance Sheet and the Net Income Statement.

Some people regard the balance sheet as an intimidating technical document, and shy clear of it, but although you may not have the accounting skill to prepare it, you can easily understand it, and it is extremely useful.

World of Gifts

BALANCE SHEET	Compiled as of: 12/31/02	12/31/01
ASSETS		
Current Assets		
Cash	3,045	1,163
Inventory	185,394	146,546
Deposits and prepayments	1,168	2,089
Employee Salary Advances	2,314	18,797
Total Current Assets	**191,921**	**168,595**
Fixed Assets		
Furniture, Fixtures and Equipment	58,860	40,773
Less: Accumulated Depreciation	(31,499)	(25.404)
Net Fixed Assets	27,361	15,369
A. Total Assets at Cost	***219,282***	***183,964***
LIABILITIES and OWNERS' EQUITY		
Current Liabilities		
Accounts Payable	62,488	53,477
Accrued Taxes and Expenses	4,737	4,153
Long Term Debt: Current Portion	5,700	– 0 –
Total Current Liabilities	72,925	57,630
Long Term Debt		
Long Term Debt	9,258	
Less: Current Portion	(5,700)	
	3,558	
Deferred Income Taxes	1,500	
	5,058	
B. Total Liabilities	**77,983**	**57,630**
Owner's Equity		
Retained Earnings, beginning of year	116,333	99,975
Net Income during year	14,965	16,358
Retained Earnings, end of year	131,298	116,333
Capital Stock	10,001	10,001
C. Total Owners' Equity	**141,299**	**126,334**
D. Total Liabilities & Owners' Equity	***219,282***	***183,964***

Unlike the **Net Income Statement**, which records the flow of revenues and expenses over a period of time, the Balance Sheet describes the financial condition of the whole business at a given moment (usually the last day of the *fiscal year*), by comparing assets (all that the business owns or is owed) with *liabilities* (all that the business owes). The balance sheet for a small gift shop might look like the example on the previous page.

Assets are balanced against **Liabilities** and **Owner's Equity**, hence the term Balance Sheet. Another way of putting it is to say that **Owners' Equity** is the surplus of **Assets** over **Liabilities**. It may seem odd to include the Owner's Equity on the Liabilities side, but it is owed to him by the business, so for the business it is indeed a Liability.

Owners' Equity is not, of course, calculated by simply subtracting **Liabilities from Assets**. It will probably consist of Capital Stock (if, as in this case, the business is a corporation), plus **Accumulated Earnings** from previous years, plus the **Net Income** (Retained Earnings) from the current year's **Net Income Statement**. This demonstrates the self-checking element in bookkeeping: the sum of those amounts must equal the difference between **Assets** and **Liabilities**.

Let us see how we can use this Balance Sheet in managing the business:

Assets

Current Assets:
Inventory has gone up 26.51%, but **Employee Salary Advances** (an asset because they are owed to the business) have decreased about $16,000, so the total increase in **Current Assets** is only 13.84%. If we calculate **Current Assets** leaving out **Salary Advances** in both years, we see an increase of 26.58%. Needless to say, borrowing money from the business is not a good way to increase the **Assets**, and these figures show the importance of looking behind the totals.

Fixed Assets:
Furniture and Fixtures have increased by about $18,000. This would be explained in the **Notes**, and we will assume that it was the purchase of a fully integrated computer system (these accounts must have been generated when computers were more expensive). Accumulated **Depreciation** increases by this item's depreciation for the year.

Liabilities and Owner's Equity

Current Liabilities:
Accounts Payable have increased slightly. We will look at **Sales** in the **Income Statement** to see whether it is a manageable amount. **Accrued Taxes** are stable, and the current portion of long-term debt will be part of the computer purchase.
Long Term Debt will be the balance owed on the computer system.

Owner's Equity:
(**Retained Earnings** plus **Net Income** for the current year, plus **Capital Stock**) is up, but is less than it should be **because Net Income** has dropped 8.52%.

Look, however, at the fourth line from the end of the *Net Income Statement* on the following page.

The fall in **Net Income** of 8.52% is due largely to a huge increase in **Interest Expense**, $13,240 against last year's $3,041.

That does seem a high figure for interest payments, and if we were analyzing these accounts more deeply we would find out exactly what they served. Giving management the benefit of the doubt, we may guess that the effect, which is reduction of income tax liability, was intended, as without the interest payments, Income Tax would have been payable on the $30,038 **Net Operating Income**.

Although this 34.78% increase looks excellent, we should not be satisfied with it, because it was achieved solely because Sales were up 18%, and **Cost of Goods Sold** down by 2.66%, which offset a shocking increase in expenses of 24.95%. In other words, Management concentrated successfully on two of the factors required for growth, but lost control of the vital third one, expenses.

Returning to the Balance Sheet, the increase of $6,000 in **Depreciation** is, of course, a consequence of the increase in **Fixed Assets**.

Looking at **Liabilities**, we see that **Accounts Payable** (outstanding debts for merchandise) have gone up 16.85%, to $62,488, but **Sales** are up more, by 18.38%, which on the face of it is satisfactory.

Average monthly sales last year, however, were only $63,072.08, and if the coming month follows suit that will be barely enough to cover the $62,488 of payables (which will mostly be on 30 day terms), with nothing left over for operating expenses.

World of Gifts

Net Income Statement

Compiled for Fiscal Years ended _______

	This Year	Last Year	% of
SALES	**756,865**	**639,357**	**100.00%**
Cost of Goods Sold	413,193	366,054	54.59%
GROSS PROFIT	**343,672**	**273,303**	**45.41%**
Expenses			0.00%
Advertising	15,132	18,229	2.00%
Auto and Delivery	11		0.00%
Bad Debts		263	
Bank Charges	299	161	0.04%
Contributions	726	1,255	0.10%
Commissions and Contract Labor	449	1,235	0.06%
Depreciation and Amortization	6,095	4,227	0.81%
Dues and Subscriptions	1,971	1,366	0.26%
Entertainment and Travel	11,303	5,777	1.49%
Insurance	14,088	9,923	1.86%
Over/Short	96	23	0.01%
Office Supplies	12,185	9,692	1.61%
Professional Fees	4,457	3,432	0.59%
Salaries – Officers	57,711	63,100	7.63%
– Other	86,308	63,660	11.40%
Sales Expense	10,624	7,555	1.40%
Rent	43,200	41,800	5.71%
Repairs	1,538	2,150	0.20%
Taxes	35,201	8,193	4.65%
Utilities	12,240	8,976	1.62%
Total Expenses	**313,634**	**251,017**	**41.44%**
Net Operating Income	**30,038**	**22,286**	**3.97%**
(Gross Profit less Expenses)			
Interest Expense	13,240	3,041	1.75%
Net Income before Income Taxes	16,798	19,245	2.22%
Provision for Income Tax	1,833	2,887	0.24%
NET INCOME	**14,965**	**16,358**	**1.98%**

The sales required are what the payables are 54.59% of (last year's **Cost of Goods Sold**), which is $114,467.85.

This demonstrates the function of Working Capital. The **Accounts Payable** may have been deliberately incurred to increase **inventory** for a Special Event or seasonal sales burst, with all obligations provided for in the **Cash Flow Forecast. Working Capital** will meet operating expenses for the time being, and will be replenished by coming sales increases.

The full interpretation of the Balance Sheet will depend upon more factors than we have space to discuss here, but you can see that by examining and questioning it in detail, with its companion Income statement, you can give your business a thorough physical, judging the effect of previous decisions, and prescribing future treatment. Furthermore, if you go to the bank for a loan, a thorough understanding of the balance sheet will enable you to discuss it with your loan officer on more than equal terms, so that if, for instance, he finds what he thinks is a weakness, you will be able either to explain it, or describe the remedy which you will already have started to apply. As I point out at every opportunity, your Accounts are your basic tool of management – do not ever regard them as merely an evil necessity to satisfy the IRS.

While the Balance Sheet is essential for long-term planning, the Net Income Statement is the control tool for day to day management. It is mandatory once a year (for the Income Tax return), but if possible it should also be prepared monthly and quarterly (if bookkeeping is computerized, it can be brought up daily). This not only provides the figures for Sales Tax and for the quarterly Form 1020 for Estimated Income Tax (avoiding either penalty or overpayment), but also gives a constant check on expenses.

Cost of Goods Sold in the annual Income Statement will be based on physical inventory count, but for interim Statements (if you are not fully computerized) it can be the percentage of **Gross Sales** from the last annual Statement.

In a gift shop one might, for instance, make an interim Statement at September 30th, which would be three-quarters of the way through the calendar year, but only half-way in the year's Gross Sales, as the fourth quarter typically accounts for half a gift shop's annual gross (and often half of that in December alone).

Interim Net Income Statement
September 30, 1998

	This Year to Date	% of Sales	Last Year to Date	% of Sales
GROSS SALES	60,000		58,000	
Less Cost of Goods Sold:				
Opening Inventory			18,000	
Plus Purchases			31,000	
			49,000	
Less Closing Inventory			15,940	
Cost of Goods Sold (this year assume last year's 57%)	34,200	57%	33,060	57%
Gross Profit	25,800	43%	24,940	43%
Less Expenses (itemized)	28,800	48%	29,580	51%
NET INCOME before tax	(3,000)		(4,640)	

(Last year's figures, and the percentages, are essential, as performance can only be judged by comparison).

Negative Net Income is not unusual at this time of year (which is why Cash Flow Forecast – *which see* – is so important), but the picture will change dramatically by year's end, as the final three months will add another $60,000 and there will be very little change in the percentage of Expenses. As long as Inventory is under control the year should end up like this:

Gross Sales whole year	120,000
Gross Profit 43%	51,600
Expenses 48%	57,600
NET INCOME	6,000 (5% of Gross Sales)

Not that 5% of Sales is a Net Income to be proud of, but we may deliberately have been increasing Advertising or the payroll to reduce corporate income tax. If not, we may have to look very closely at Inventory, Expenses, and Sales strategy for the last quarter, to see if we can improve matters.

FINANCIAL YEAR: If you open for business on, say, 16th October, your Financial Year will run from 1st October to 30th September. You can leave it at that, or change it subject to some restrictions depending upon the exact nature of the corporation: consult your CPA. You must, however, file a tax return to define it. If, for instance, having started in October, you wanted to go to the calendar financial year, you would file a "short year" tax return for October, November and December, taking inventory on 31st December. Whatever the financial year, it will be necessary to take physical inventory on the last day, because the critical **Cost of Goods Sold** figure in the Net Income Statement relies on opening and closing inventories.

The choice of financial year depends upon the nature of the business and the personal preference of the owner, the decision resting largely on the easiest and most convenient time to take inventory. A gift shop, for instance, will probably have the lowest inventory on 31st. December, just after the strongest selling season of the year. The owner may, however, feel that the extra work of taking inventory so soon after a hectic Christmas season is unacceptable, and opt for a mid-year date, when inventory will also be fairly low, being a comparatively slow time of year, and too early for any Christmas build-up.

It is generally preferable to match the financial to the calendar year, otherwise an undefined "year" can be either, causing confusion in one's own thinking, let alone in conversation.

FINANCING A BUSINESS: There are several ways to finance a business, and they can be used singly or together.

- Your own money
- A bank loan against your own Collateral
- Loans from family and friends
- Bank loans with family or friends as cosigners

- An SBA (Small Business Administration) loan
- Sale of stock, if you have formed a Corporation

J. L. Garvin, a legendary British newspaper editor, once said of capitalism that it enhanced "the vigor, variety and zest of life," and that "Freedom to undertake affairs in the hope of gain and at the risk of loss is the breath and lifeblood of this system."

Banks are not very keen on the vigor, variety and zest of life, and they are certainly not interested in the risk of loss, so you will have to be very persuasive to raise capital needed for premises, equipment and inventory, and to cover operating losses for the first year or two. For this purpose the business plan is essential.

Even if you are relying on private investors, or using your own money (and these are the sources of capital for most small businesses), you will not be able to say how much is needed, let alone persuade other people to invest, without a business plan, and buyers of stock will want to see one too.

The SBA does not, except in a few exceptional cases, make loans itself, nor does it offer unusually low interest rates. It guarantees bank loans, and can obtain longer repayment terms than would otherwise be possible.

See Business Plan, Collateral, Equity and Debt, Loan, SBA, S.C.O.R.E.

FISCAL YEAR: Same as Financial Year, *which see.*

FIXED AND UNFIXED EXPENSE: Some bookkeeping manuals divide Expenses into Fixed and Unfixed, which is confusing, because Fixed does not mean that it never changes, but that it is mandatory, like Rent, which has to be paid just to keep the doors open. Advertising, on the other hand, would be called an Unfixed expense, because it is discretionary – you do not have to spend anything at all on it if you do not want to.

FLOAT: The cash in the register at start of business is the Float. It should be a fixed amount, unchanged from day to day. A typical starting float for a small store might be $150, consisting of two rolls each of pennies, nickels, dimes and quarters (one loose and one in reserve), 50 one-dollar bills, 7 five-dollar bills, and 3 ten-dollar bills. The actual mix will depend on experience.

FLOOR. The interior design of the store is critical to your success, and the choice of floor is critical to the success of any design concept. The choice is confined to carpet, vinyl tile, hardwood, and, perhaps, concrete. All have specific advantages of cost, suitability, appearance, utility, durability, and ease of maintenance, and the choice will finally fall on the material best suited to your particular needs and Budget.

Carpet imparts a wonderful air of luxury, but will show wear on the footways, and repositioning of display units is extremely difficult, as it is virtually impossible to slide them, and they leave long-lasting indentations in the pile. It is quite expensive, and not as long-lasting as other materials. Carpet also has to be vacuumed every day, which because of the noise, should be done out of hours, while hard floors can be swept less obtrusively.

Vinyl tile is extremely smart, and comes in a huge variety of patterns, while wood parquet (which also comes in tile form) creates a warmer and more intimate atmosphere.

Both wood and vinyl tile, apart from being easy to maintain, make changing the store layout simple, because measurements can be made just by counting tiles (usually 12" square), and display units can be moved around with ease. If your original plan was based on mostly free-standing display units rather than built-in or fixed furniture, this will save much trouble and expensive re-modeling.

For some types of store, concrete is excellent provided it is in good condition, sealed and painted. This is the cheapest of all floors, and if not suitable for a whole store, may well be ideal for part, and certainly for the stock room.

Whatever you do, do not take the floor for granted. Choose it, and maintain it, with care; its character and condition are vital elements in the Image of the store.

FLOOR LIMIT. In the days of hand imprinting, credit card companies used to set a Floor Limit of perhaps $50 or $75, above which you were required to telephone for authorization of the transaction, but the now almost universal electronic processing incorporates automatic authorization. If the card company does need reassurance, the display screen on the terminal will say so, and tell you what to do.

FLOOR PLAN: The percentage of rented space taken up by non-productive bathroom, office, back-room, lunch space, and sales area (cash register etc.) must be kept to an absolute minimum, and this cannot be achieved unless you have a scale plan of the whole premises. The bathroom is probably not negotiable (save for total size and the position of the door), as the cost of moving the plumbing is prohibitive. The size of the Backroom and Sales Area will depend on the type of business, but offices are fairly standard in their requirements: 108 sq. ft. (9' × 12') is commonly acceptable, and is enough for two desks, one for a computer and printer, plus copy machine, filing cabinet, fax, telephones, storage cabinet and bookshelf. It should have easy access to the showroom, and if possible a one-way mirror or a window, so that you can see the showroom and the front door from your desk.

The back-room, containing the shipping and receiving tables, can be small if it is kept tidy, and if it is possible to maintain a "little and often" purchasing policy. There will always be some inventory in the back-room, but the constant aim should be to have none. Your money should be in the showroom or in the bank. There are no sales in the back-room.

The Sales Area, again, can be small if tidy and well laid-out. An island can be attractive, but claims walkspace all round it. With its back to a wall, it needs walkspace only in front. Its position in the store should be sufficiently close to the door for the cashier to keep an eye on comings and goings, but not so close as to be a target of opportunity for passing robbers, or to make it difficult to see the rest of the store.

The lay-out of the showroom itself will depend entirely on the type of business. One may need a crowded effect, with massed merchandise and narrow aisles (but leave room for wheelchairs and for merchandise trolleys), while another may need spacious elegance (but don't overdo it; the display units pay the rent, not the floor in between).

No draftsman's skill is needed to make a good plan, as you can get large paper ruled in ¼" squares. At one inch to the foot, three inches per square, there is no guesswork.

FREIGHT: Control of freight costs is critically important, because Freight is included in the cost of the merchandise: it is not an Expense. As mentioned under costing, if you buy something for a dollar, net, plus 5 cents freight, its cost to you is $1.05, and at Keystone, its Retail will be $2.10. If, on the other hand, you buy at $2.00 List, less 50%, with 5 cents freight, the Retail has to be $2.00, but the cost to you is $1.05, and your profit, instead of being a clear 50% Keystone, becomes 95 cents instead of a dollar, 47.5% instead of 50%. Take advantage whenever possible of special offers which include free freight, and of all Freight Allowances.

FREIGHT ALLOWANCE. Vendors offer various Freight Allowances and discounts, depending on quantity, value, or weight. The most common is the provision of free freight for orders over a certain value, which can vary greatly, depending on the vendor. Another allowance is for free freight over 500 pounds, which is commonly a minimum for road freight (you can ship less, but you pay as if for 500 pounds).

You may sometimes be in such need of specific merchandise that you will place a small order, pay the freight and take a smaller Margin, rather than disappoint customers, but as a general rule always ensure that your orders are large enough to qualify for Freight Allowance, unless the quantity will overload your inventory.

Make sure that you know the rules before you order. It is particularly important to ensure that the free freight allowance applies to the amount you order, not to the amount shipped: it has been known for the order to be well above the limit, but the amount shipped to be below it, with consequent freight charge, and much ill feeling.

The vendor may pre-pay the freight for qualifying shipments, but sometimes you will pay "freight collect," or have it charged on the invoice, and you then deduct the amount if you pay on time, losing the Allowance if you are late.

There are many varieties of freight allowance, and it always pays to inquire. Some vendors regard them as a regrettable necessity, rather than an inducement, and tend not to mention them unless asked.

FURNITURE, FIXTURES & FITTINGS: This heading in the accounts will include display units, but also cash register stands, and gift-wrap tables for the showroom, plus everything in the back, such as office furniture, storage cabinets, shipping and receiving tables, back-room shelving, table, chairs and kitchen equipment for a lunch room, etc. The showroom pieces must be, like everything else in the front of the store, of a quality and design to impress customers. Nothing in the back is going to impress anybody, except the people who use it. It must, therefore, be sturdy and suitable. Shelving, for instance, should be standard industrial type, rather than the household variety obtainable in retail discount stores, and good desks, cabinets, etc., can be found at used office furniture stores. Look for quality, but there is no need to spend money on newness. *See also* Some Assembly Required.

Office furniture and equipment can also be leased, for which the payments are an Expense, rather than the capital expenditure for purchase. The decision to lease or purchase will depend on individual circumstances.

Keep a register of all Furniture, Fixtures & Fittings showing at least date of purchase and price paid. This is essential for Depreciation (*which see*) and is extremely useful if you should ever need to sell a piece.

G

GARBAGE. The amount of Garbage generated by a small retail store is astounding. You will quickly find that city pick-up (even if available to commercial premises, which it sometimes is not) is inadequate, and in any case probably requires that you put the trash on the sidewalk in front of the store, which you certainly do not want.

This means that you will probably have a dumpster, and the smaller it is and the less frequently it is serviced, the less it will cost, so always knock empty cardboard boxes flat, or fill them tight with trash, because the dumpster will quickly overflow if you simply throw in empty boxes – and if, as is quite likely, you are sharing it, you will be deservedly unpopular.

Make sure, too, that discarded packing materials are securely bagged. Nothing makes a place look seedy so quickly as wind-scattered plastic peanuts and crumples of paper.

If you do any shipping, save a good supply of plastic peanuts for your own use, and take advantage of any other re-cycling opportunities.

GIFT CERTIFICATES. Apart from solving gift selection problems for frustrated or unimaginative customers, Gift Certificates provide free money until they are redeemed (some may even be forgotten), and they may also introduce the recipient to the store for the first time, gaining you a new customer. They are particularly useful as Charitable Donations because they avoid the problems of selecting a suitable item, or writing a check, also the obligation is deferred until redemption, and the name of the store is mentioned loud and clear at the presentation (recognition which may be omitted if the donation is a piece of merchandise), and again, the recipient has to come into the store, perhaps for the first time.

You may want to put on an expiration date, but enforcing it can lead to bad feeling if the Certificate has simply been mislaid.

A custom-printed Certificate bearing your Logo is preferable, if the budget will run to it, but standard Gift Certificates are available from most office supply stores, usually in check-book form, with matching envelopes and a stub for store records.

If your computer is up to it, you can produce very attractive Gift Certificates yourself, but these will not have the "check-stub" or carbon duplicate format of the store-bought variety, and you will have to devise your own register of certificates sold.

GIFT REGISTRY: *see* Bridal Registry.

GIFT WRAP. The offer of free Gift Wrap will close many a doubtful sale, will often add another little purchase just to fill up the box, will positively attract people to your store in preference to others which charge for, or do not provide, Gift Wrap, and the wrap itself will advertise your store to the recipient. The cost of Gift Wrap materials can be charged against Selling Expense or Advertising, my own feeling being that it truly belongs in the latter.

The Gift Wrap table should be adjacent to the cash register, so that the cashier can double as Gift Wrapper. Only large stores can afford the staff for a separate Gift Wrap counter (unless you decide to go the opposite route, and aggressively sell Gift Wrap service, with prices and elaborateness to match). The Gift Wrap table must be big enough for two people to work at once, as you may need extra help at peak periods.

Gift Wrap materials and equipment are available from several sources, such as the major paper companies (if there is one in your city you may be able to save money by picking up your order at the warehouse), from local distributors, from Brokers in your nearest Trade Center, and direct from the manufacturers. Your choice will depend upon your needs, your budget, and your location.

The specialist Gift Wrap companies are the most convenient source for everything you need, as they supply not only an enormous variety of Gift Boxes in every conceivable shape and size (with, in their catalogs, suggested uses for each), but also an equal variety of Gift Wrap paper in large rolls, plus ribbon, tie cord, bows, paper dispensers to hold the rolls, and custom benches in several sizes, to hold the more popular selections of Gift Boxes.

You will have the choice of Gift Boxes printed with your name and Logo, or plain. You may find it better to have them plain (which is a little cheaper) as the printing will be covered if the box is wrapped, and your attractive custom label can always be put on either box or wrap. (You will sometimes need a plain box, too, for the customer, usually a man, who should have bought the gift while he was out of town on a trip)

GRAND OPENING: Do not rush it. You do not want to cope with such a critically important Event – or indeed any event at all – on the first day, or even in the first week, of business. You need what ship-builders call a shake-down cruise before you commit yourself to advertising and sending out invitations. You may even find, if you are happily busy in the first few weeks, and business is up to projections, that the time, trouble and expense of mounting a Grand Opening are not justified. There is a fine line to be drawn here, between being too easily satisfied on the one hand, and advertising for its own sake on the other.

GROSS PROFIT: In Accounts, Gross Profit is what is left from Gross Sales after paying for the goods sold (*see* Cost of Goods Sold). On individual items, it is the difference between TDC (True Delivered Cost), and Retail Price (*see* Costing).

GROSS SALES: The term can be deceptive. It used to mean all sales before deducting returns etc., but now that cash registers do all such deductions automatically, and print what is in fact a Net figure for the day's sales, that figure is sometimes called Gross because it is final. Once again, the meaning of an apparently simple business term depends upon who is talking.

It must not be confused with Gross Income, which includes non-sales items such as payments for insurance claims, or cash refunds from vendors.

It is dangerously easy to think of the Bank Deposit, which includes Sales Tax, as Gross Sales, which do not. With 8% Sales Tax, for instance, a satisfying Bank Deposit of $1,000 including tax, means Gross

Sales of only $925.93. *See also* Net Sales.

GROWTH: The only Growth that counts is Growth of Net Income. Without enlarging the premises, this can be achieved by:

- increasing Gross Profit on unchanged or growing Gross Sales, provided Expenses are not increasing.
- increasing Gross Sales on unchanged or growing Gross Profit, again provided that Expenses are not increasing.
- reducing Expenses, provided neither Sales or Gross Profit are falling.

In other words, the constant aim must be to increase Sales and Gross Profit while reducing Expenses.

If Growth is to be achieved by enlarging the premises, comparisons with previous years in the old premises will be in the form of ratios, rather than dollar amounts. If Gross Profit, for instance, was 45%, it must remain at that or improve, and Expenses as a percentage of Gross Sales must not increase, even if rent per square foot and other expenses rise.

Dollar sales per square foot, however, remain valid for comparison if rent per square foot does not change. If it rises, expenses will rise out of proportion to the physical increase. It will then be necessary to recalculate the break even point, and dollar comparisons per square foot will no longer be valid.

Warning: Put the Net Income to good tax-deductible use during the year, for increased owner's salary, dividends, or such other worthwhile purpose as your CPA recommends, so that it does not end up as taxable Net Income on the Federal Income Tax return. This can only be done by monitoring Monthly Net Income, for which Cost of Goods Sold must be known, for which in turn an Inventory figure is necessary, and that figure is not available without computerized Inventory Control. *See* Computers *and* Cost of Goods Sold.

H

HANDICAPPED: It is a policy of enlightened self-interest, to say the least, to provide for the handicapped. Inside the store the floor plan should be convenient for people in wheelchairs, and for two people abreast, so that a frail customer can rely on a companion for support. There may also be city codes to be complied with. Your efforts, however, will be largely wasted if access from the parking lot is awkward, in which case you may have to ask the landlord to provide a ramp up a sidewalk curb, modify steps, or do whatever else is necessary.

Consider, too, the advantages of employing handicapped staff, who must first have unusual determination to have overcome their handicap, and secondly tend to be very reliable, as their job security is even more important to them than to most of us.

S.C.O.R.E., the Service Corps for Retired Executives

HELP. A business and its owner will always, from the first day, have questions and problems, about everything from simple procedures to major decisions on policy and financing. Help is always available.

The most comprehensive and expert source of free help is SCORE, the Senior Corps of Retired Executives (http://score.org/). It is under the wing of the Small Business Administration, and is staffed by volunteer retired executives with the broadest possible spectrum of experience. Whatever the nature of your business, there will be someone there with knowledge of all its aspects, from initial planning and financing, to daily operation, to expansion. Many SCORE chapters run excellent seminars on running your own business, and their offices have comprehensive reference libraries and helpful computer programs. For full information, and the address of your nearest branch, write to SCORE, 655 15th Street, NW, Suite 910, Washington DC, 20005-5742. Local offices are in the phone book under Small Business Administration, in the Government pages.

City Hall may well have a "one-stop" help office, to guide entrepreneurs through local and state permit and tax return requirements, the Chamber of Commerce will have valuable resources, and the IRS run useful tax seminars.

For self-help, the public library is unrivaled, and librarians always seem pleased to guide one's search; furthermore, do not hesitate to ask local, state or federal bureaucrats for assistance; they all seem glad of the chance to show that bureaucracy's somewhat tarnished reputation is undeserved.

HOLD: Customers often ask for an item to be held for them. Depending on what it is, and how long it is to be held, this does not usually present any problem, provided you follow a simple drill:

1. **Take the customer's name and telephone number.**

2. **Note the date through which the item is to be held.**

3. **Show whether the item has been paid for.**

4. **Put the item on a dedicated "Hold Shelf," so that it can readily be found if the person who took the hold is out.**

5. **Tape the paper showing this information onto the item.**

It takes a surprisingly short time for unlabelled or undated "hold" items to accumulate and cause problems. It is infuriating to have valuable stock on the hold shelf with no date, and even worse not to find a hold item when the customer comes in for it.

HOLD-UP: Shopping centers in even the most respectable neighborhoods can be targets for armed robbery. Professional advice, if someone points a gun at you and demands the money, is to give it to him without delay, and avoid looking at him, so that he will not think you are hoping to identify him later. There is no point in doing anything else: he is fully prepared, you are not; he has a gun in his hand and you do not. Train the staff accordingly, and hope it never happens.

HOLIDAYS: Do not be casual about holiday entitlement. As owner you will probably have time off as and when you can, but your employees, even if they are as much friends as employees, need clear-cut rules as to how much time off they can expect, and how much latitude they have in deciding when to go. It is important to fix the holiday schedule as early in the year as possible, making sure that it does not conflict with any local events which may make extra demands on staff, or Special Events which you may have planned yourself.

The schedule cannot be rigid, but it must be there, so that if one person has to change dates the effects on others can be seen at once, and arrangements made accordingly.

HOURS OF BUSINESS: Your business hours will depend on the type of business, the location, the clientele, and the hours of the stores around you (unless you are in a mall, when the lease will require that you keep mall hours). In some locations it pays to stay open late one night a week (usually Thursday); in others it may be necessary to stay open until 9 p.m. every night, and in others 9 to 6 may be just right, with perhaps 12 to 5 on Sundays. This is a decision which can only be made case by case, but it should be made on the basis of what will most benefit the store, rather than on the preferred getting-up time of the owner. I have a personal preference for 9 a.m. opening rather than the more common 10 a.m., as although business may be slow for the first hour, the customers will be delighted that you are open when others are not, and it gives time for straightening the shelves and making other preparations for the day.

At Christmas time many stores will stay open late during December, perhaps until 8 p.m. Monday through Friday, but with regular weekend hours – and opening on Sundays if they have not done so during the year.

HUMAN RESOURCES: *see* Employee Leasing, Job Satisfaction, *and* Personnel.

I

IMAGE: The Image of your store is the projection of its personality, which is bound to be at least in part a projection of your own. Like you, it will express its personality through appearance and behavior. Just as the first impression you make on others depends on your clothes and how you wear them, so your store's first (and critically important) impression on customers depends on the merchandise and how it is displayed. Even the finest merchandise will not realize its full potential if not displayed to best advantage, and this will depend not only on the units upon which it is shown but also on the basic design and decor of the whole store.

You may be able to decide objectively on the sort of image you want, and deliberately build it into your initial planning. Logo, store design, layout, merchandise mix, stationery, and all the rest, meticulously coordinated in advance with your business plan, budget, and sales projections.

On the other hand you may proceed much more intuitively, basing decisions on instinct and taste as you go along. There will come a point at which you will have created, all unwittingly, a firm Image. Now is the time to step back, and try to see yourself as others see you. There will be weak points, and strong ones; consistencies and contradictions. Analyze your sales; walk around the store; review your advertising, your stationery and business cards, your gift wrap and your window display. Put every aspect of your business into one frame, judge the resulting picture like a critical stranger, and make whatever changes may be needed to convey a clear consistent Image.

So much for appearance. Equally important is behavior. Just as a person may be immaculately and expensively dressed but shunned by all for surliness and bad manners, so can a shop full of perfect roses be shunned if the staff behave like thorns. On the other hand, thoughtful, well-trained staff can do a great deal to overcome faults in appearance. The best Image is one of helpful friendliness and professional competence: even glamorous charm is not enough: other things being equal, customers will choose professionalism over charm every time (with both, of course, you can't lose).

The external Image, projected through your Advertising, is discussed under that heading (*which see*).

IMPORTER: There are, broadly speaking, three types of import company. One will have goods manufactured overseas but bearing its own name, a second will select goods from around the world on their merits, sometimes benefiting from the name of a famous foreign maker, and the third will be the wholly-owned subsidiary of a foreign manufacturer.

As to the first: all imports must, by law, be labeled with the country of origin, but no law requires the maker's name. Many foreign factories will, for a sufficiently large order, put the name of the Importer on their wares, rather than their own. This is not to deceive, but to create, for the Importer of a broad range of goods, loyalty to his brand-name. The name may simply be put on a standard production item, but sometimes the Importer will have an item of his own design manufactured under contract, which has the advantage that he can change manufacturers if necessary.

The name of the second type of Importer, who selects goods from around the world, will not be known to the public. He relies on the reputation and quality of the goods themselves. He may have exclusive rights to a name already well known, or he may find a hitherto unknown, or new, product which he judges good enough to create its own reputation. He will, at the same time, market more ordinary products which will sell on their own merits regardless of name.

From the point of view of the imaginative or inquisitive retailer, import companies have one great defect: they import only a selection of the manufacturer's wares. A visit to the foreign factory or showroom will almost certainly reveal a treasury of items which the importer has not selected, but which the visiting retailer will judge to be potential best-sellers. This does not mean that the importer was wrong to shun them. He has to select an average to please a very broad market. The individual retailer, on the other hand, knows a narrower market more deeply, and may do very well with an item which would fail elsewhere. Whether the manufacturer will agree to sell such items direct to the retailer will depend entirely on the nature of his agreement with the importer. Sometimes there is no problem, and sometimes the importer may have exclusive rights, even if he chooses not to use the whole of the manufacturer's range. This is a matter for individual negotiation.

The third type of importer is the wholly owned subsidiary of a foreign maker. Just like other importers, such subsidiaries bring in only a selection of what is available. They will not normally accept special orders for anything else, and it is unlikely that the parent factory will export direct to a retailer, but it's always worth asking.

Well-traveled customers have often asked me why such-and-such a manufacturer does not export a particular item. The answer is that he may have tried to, but the importer chose not to buy it. It is more true to say that importers import, rather than that manufacturers export. Even wholly owned foreign subsidiaries usually import, telling the home factory what they want, rather than the home factory exporting, and sending what they think they should have (although there are home factories which claim to know the market better than their representatives on the spot!).

IMPORTING: Apart from advantages mentioned above of finding items not handled by wholesale importers, direct import has the even stronger advantage of giving the retailer access to excellent merchandise which, if it had to carry a middleman importer's profit, would be priced out of the market, but if imported direct can be sold at a competitive price, and is also probably unobtainable elsewhere.

Many people find the idea of direct import rather daunting, believing that manufacturers will insist on impossibly large orders, and that the whole import business is fraught with difficulties involving currency exchange rates, licenses, customs duties, and all sorts of other shadowy threats and hassles. Like any other problem, it becomes simple if taken one step at a time.

First, deal with the manufacturer on his own turf. Meet him at an international trade show, such as the International Spring Fair at Birmingham in England, or the similar and even larger one at Frankfurt. You will indeed meet some manufacturers who talk in nothing less than container loads, but there are many more who will gladly accept order for under $1000, and who are well versed in the best shipping method. One of the most useful methods is "Informal Entry." The goods are sent by Air Parcel Post (not Air Freight), with a label showing contents and value. For most types of product, provided the value is less than $1,000, U.S. Customs will assess the Duty (if any), and this will be collected, with a small fee, by the postman when he brings the parcel into the store. Air Parcel Post is expensive, but it eliminates Custom House Brokers' fees, which, apart from being large, can also be unpredictable.

For larger orders, or for items simply not suitable for Air Parcel Post, Air or Sea freight is not difficult to arrange. The foreign manufacturer will probably be able to recommend a Freight Forwarder, who will be accustomed to filling containers with consolidated shipments from several different manufacturers, for several different customers. The Custom House Brokers at your nearest port will be listed in the Yellow Pages, and your Freight Forwarder may have a working relationship with one of them, which simplifies matters a little. There will usually be only three bills to pay: one to the manufacturer (you can get a bank draft in his currency from Thomas Cook Foreign Currency Services, which is easier and cheaper than a wire transfer from a bank), one to the local Custom House Broker (which will include payment for the Freight Forwarder, the U.S. Customs, and himself), and one to the freight company which bring the goods to the store. You often make two payments for domestic shipments anyway – to the vendor and to the freight company – so the only extra payment for direct import is to the Custom House Broker.

For full information on import regulations, restrictions and duties, I have always found U.S. Customs very helpful, and, of course, Custom House Brokers also have all the information you need. Check with both Customs and Broker for duty and freight charges before you confirm an order, so that you are not taken by expensive surprise after the goods have arrived.

Companies such as Federal Express offer good service, but the bill for customs duty usually arrives some considerable time after the goods, so accurate costing can be delayed. Either you guess at it and hope you are neither over nor under pricing, or the goods stay unprofitably in the stock room until the duty is known.

INCENTIVES: As owner, your incentive is simply the success of the business, which will increase your net worth and your income. As you will not succeed without the help of colleagues and staff, it is at the very least a policy of enlightened self-interest to give them an opportunity to share in that success, by providing some form of incentive. The structure of any incentive plan in a small store with few employees must be tailored to the people involved, but whatever is decided must be fully defined and clearly explained. "We'll see what we can do about a bonus if we have a good Christmas" is not sufficient.

Some incentive plans:

- Fixed-sum bonuses for percentage increases in sales or net income (*e.g.* $50 if last month's sales were 10% or more above last year). This does not necessarily mean that you have to reveal the actual amount of sales or net income.

- Profit Sharing: a percentage of the month's, quarter's or year's net income. If you value your financial privacy, this will not do. On the other hand, complete openness about the store's finances may in itself be an excellent way to build morale and loyalty. *See* Profit Sharing.

- Individual sales commissions do not involve revealing any business results, but are the least satisfactory. The salesperson has to remember to press a button or insert a key in the register, so that the sale will be credited to him or her; the lure of a commission may lead to unseemly competition for customers; and there may be squabbles about whose sale it really was. The salesperson's hope of commission may also lead to customers being upset by over-zealous sales-manship.

All incentive plans (except commission sales) suffer from the funda-mental problem that the amount depends more upon management rather than on the direct efforts of the beneficiaries, and payments can go down as well as up. This can cause discontent unless the structure of the plan is fully explained and clearly understood at the beginning.

INCOME TAX. You are in the business to make a profit – Net Income – but do not let it accumulate during the year, until it finishes up on the Income Tax return, where much of it will be sacrificed to the government. Put it to good tax-deductible use during the year, for increased owner's salary, dividends, or such other good purpose as your CPA recommends. This can only be done by monitoring a monthly Net Income Statement, for which Cost of Goods Sold must be known, for which in turn an Inventory figure is necessary, and that figure is not available without computerized Inventory Control. *See* Computers *and* Cost of Goods Sold.

INSURANCE: Think how often you have seen a report of a small business destroyed by fire or storm, with the sad ending "the owner was not insured." Running a business without insurance is like driving across Death Valley without a spare wheel or a water bottle.

The best insurance is probably what your agent will call an "all-risk" policy. Do not, however, assume that "all-risk" means what it says. As retailers, for instance, we might reasonably expect it to include the shop windows, but it probably does not.

Discuss with your agent what is included, which will most likely be the normal storm, theft and vandalism, as well as fire. Add or subtract coverage until you have what you need, and remember, if you are in a flood-prone area, that flood insurance is separate.

Liability insurance is usually thought of as protection against accidents, such as a customer slipping and hurting herself in the store, but a good policy will also protect against other perils, such as a lawsuit filed against a retailer by a malicious ex-colleague. The insurance company will nominate an attorney and cover the cost.

INTERNET: *See* World Wide Web.

INVENTORY: If you have the right inventory at the right price in the right quantities at the right time, you are a genius.

- **The Right Inventory** is merchandise which sells fast at a high profit.

- **The Right Price** is the price which will yield maximum profit without discouraging sales.

- **The Right Quantity** is the quantity sufficient to maintain maximum rate of sale on minimum inventory.

- **The Right Time** is the period in which Sales ride the wave-crest of fashion, fad, or season.

Right Inventory

Inventory which will sell fast at a high profit is the ideal, but there will always be a trade-off between speed and profit. If you sell one hundred items at $5 each you will gross $500, and at 40% profit you will earn $200 (you have spent $300 to get $200). If, on the other hand, you sell four items at $100 each you will only gross $400, but if the profit is 50% you will again earn $200, but will have spent only $200 to get it. If, however, you sell *two* hundred of the $5 items *in the same time period*, you have twice the cash on the lower profit margin.

This also shows how Gross Sales figures alone can be misleading: $500 a day looks a lot better than $400, but if the $500 is at 40%, and the $400 at 50%, you gain more from the lower figure because you have spent less for the same profit. Always monitor your profit margins.

Right Price

You may not have much freedom in fixing your retail prices, as you are often confined by vendors' recommended retails, and by local competition. There may, however, be considerable flexibility in the purchase price. Factors which can reduce the purchase price are choice of Vendor (an actual example is a teapot listed at $24 by one vendor, and at $18.75 by another; a difference, at keystone, of $10.50 in the retail price). Show Specials (such as 10% off if you order at the Trade Show); Vendors' Seasonal Sales and Promotions (dinnerware commonly goes on Sale in the Spring and Fall); Quantity Discounts; Special Offers; Prompt Payment Discount (2% 10 days, Net 30); Free Freight over a certain order value; Freight Allowance for prompt payment, and dating (deferred payment, enabling you to sell all the merchandise – you hope – before you have to pay for it. The price is not reduced, but you get the use of the money in the meantime).

If you have a unique product, with no vendor's "suggested retail price" and no direct competition, you may charge what the market will bear, setting price and profit margin to achieve the rate of sale you need.

Right Quantity

The right Quantity depends on the type of merchandise, the rate of sale, availability, terms of payment, freight costs, and the season of the year.

For year-round merchandise, order as little and as often as possible, within vendors' minimums, and at reasonable freight costs. If the terms are Net 30, and you mark up at keystone, you need sell only half the merchandise within the thirty days to make timely payment, so adjust your quantities and your ordering frequency accordingly. If your rate of sale justifies it, place orders weekly: the more frequent the orders, the more even the cash flow.

For seasonal merchandise, judging the right quantity is like handicapping a horse race. If you get it right you will sell the last seasonal item on the last day of the season – the last Christmas Card to your last customer on Christmas Eve. You may have to order early for seasonal goods, and not always with any specially favorable terms, but if your quantities are right, it is well worth the temporary financial strain.

Freight costs will to a large extent determine the size (and thus the frequency) of shipments, and the choice of shipper, which should be one that achieves the lowest breakage rate for the lowest cost. If the shipment is "fgt. pd." cost is of course not a factor, but breakage is: check all shipments carefully, and make claims promptly. Unclaimed shipping losses can erode your Gross Profit badly.

As to availability, make sure when you place the order that the goods will be available when you want them. There is nothing more infuriating than having a planned buying program dry up half-way through, unless perhaps it is the program in which the early deliveries do not arrive, and the vendor tries to atone for his sin (and save his profit) by delivering the entire order at once in the final phase, when there is not time to sell it.

Terms of payment can radically affect the quantities ordered. A Christmas dating program, for instance, which gives delivery in September, but defers payment to 50% in November and 50% in December, will allow you to order in substantial quantities, because you have so much selling time before payment is due. This again is a handicapping situation. By the time the second installment falls due, you should have sold at least enough to pay both invoices, and preferably have no more than thirty days' worth of sales left, so that you have full use of the Gross Profit, and can return to normal ordering intervals.

Right Time

The Right Time to have inventory on hand is, for most items, all year round: it is a matter of quantities, rather than items. Even special Christmas items need to be carried in token quantities all year, so that when your customers start their Christmas shopping they will know you carry what they want. There are some specifically seasonal or occasional items such as Father's Day cards which should give up valuable display space when it is not their turn, but the presence of other cards on appropriate occasions will tell your customers that you will always meet their needs.

For Christmas when (for most types of store) not only is the total demand greater than at any other time of year, but the buying season longer, quantities are best increased gradually; but for the lesser festivals, such as Easter, Valentine's Day, Father's Day, Mother's Day, and Halloween, total demand is much less, and the buying season short (though for Halloween particularly it seems to be getting longer every year), so the right time to have inventory on hand for them is probably not more than four weeks ahead.

Graduation, June Brides, and even Back to School produce demand over a vague period of time, so the Right Time for inventory is more difficult to judge. All you can do is make your own arbitrary beginning and ending dates for your selling season (Back to School does not cut off the day school starts), and schedule deliveries from your suppliers at intervals, from the first day of your season to perhaps two weeks before its end.

When it comes to the whims of fad and fashion, timing is both more critical and more difficult. Fashion is not a major concern unless you carry clothing and accessories, but fad can be important. A lot of money can be made by riding the crest of demand for something like the Pet Rock of a few years ago, but it can all disappear if you overestimate the life span of the craze, and buy too much. Better to be sold out too soon than to have this sort of inventory left over.

INVOICE: This is the most important document in the whole purchasing process, which consists altogether of Purchase Order, Packing List, Invoice and Statement. The Invoice, with its relevant Purchase Order(s), is the document of record for your accounts and for tax purposes. It shows in detail what has been shipped, what you have been charged for each item, the amount of discount (if any), shipping charges (if any), terms of payment, and total amount due. It should also show your Purchase Order number, its own number, and date, and probably your Customer Number (which identifies you in the vendor's files, and which you should have ready if you call with a query). Read the Invoice carefully: the terms may allow you to deduct full or part freight if paid on time, or give you some other advantage which should not be missed.

No Invoice should be paid until it has been checked against the Purchase Order and the Packing List, to make sure that agreed terms have been met (per Purchase Order), that the correct items have been shipped (per P.O. and Packing List) and charged (per Invoice), with any discrepancies explained.

When making payment always put the Invoice numbers on the check (you may be paying several Invoices at once), and the check number on your copies of the Invoices. It is correct business practice to file Purchase Orders with the relevant paid Invoices. In a large organization this protects against fraud, but in a small company the opportunity does not exist, and the procedure can get very cumbersome if there are several deliveries over a period of time, each with its own Invoice, against one Purchase Order.

For costing purposes, it is useful to express the total due on the Invoice (including freight) as a percentage of the Gross Retail Yield (total retail if you sold everything on the invoice). This will give a running check on Cost and Gross Profit. For instance:

The invoice is for $500 goods at retail: less 50% discount = $250 net plus $7.89 UPS charge = $257.89 total invoice.

The total $257.89 is 51.58% of $500, yielding a Gross Profit of 48.42% on this Invoice.

This is the most effective way of controlling one of the two factors which make up that absolutely critical Gross Profit figure on the Income Statement. The other factor, of course, is the size of the inventory as a whole, because cost of goods sold on an Income Statement is found by taking opening inventory at cost, adding the year's purchases, and subtracting closing inventory. *See* Costing.

J – K

JOB APPLICATION. It may seem like overkill for a small store to require completion of a formal Job Application form, but it is extremely useful in building up a file of potential full time, part time and temporary staff whose qualifications can be equally compared. Use of a form also ensures that necessary information is not forgotten. *See also* Employee Records.

JOB SATISFACTION: We all know that it's hard to find good help, but we should also acknowledge that it's hard for the help to find a good boss. Wages in the retail trade are notoriously low, and you, as the store owner, must somehow create a working atmosphere which brings out the best in people, even if only to protect your own interests. Good morale will generate a friendly and cheerful atmosphere much appreciated by customers, while bad morale will have the opposite effect, not only upon customers, but also in the back room, where tired and unhappy people can make expensive mistakes.

Individuals vary so much that it is impossible to lay down rules, but attention to a few simple needs will lay a good foundation.

- Give credit where credit is due: keep your eyes open so that you notice what your employees are doing, and be quick to praise or thank for any little creative touch, such as a refreshed display, or for any helpfulness, such as sweeping the floor. Never take your employees for granted. Make them feel appreciated.

- Whatever the rate of pay, be sure that the pay checks are regular and certain. Both praise and thanks will ring hollow if the pay checks are late (and morale will suffer if there is a perception that money is short).

- Be as generous as you possibly can with health benefits. Few things are more important to the people in your employees' wage group, and their job satisfaction is closely related to the peace of mind conferred by a good health plan. (*See* Employee Leasing).

- Ensure from the start that all employees understand what is expected of them. The job description for a cashier may be precise, but in a small store everyone has to be able and willing to do everything, from checking in and pricing new merchandise to cleaning the toilets. It should be made clear to every new employee that there is one unforgivable remark: "That's not my job."

- Be clear from the start about holiday and sick-leave entitlements. They can always be varied later on a friendly basis, but the existence of a clear structure to start with provides a sound basis for discussion, and prevents any unfortunate misunderstanding.

- Make it clear that you are always available to listen to any employee's troubles, whether they concern work or home. You may or may not be able to help, but the knowledge that you are prepared to do what you can is a valuable reassurance. Something as simple as arranging a ride to and from work for an employee with car trouble is enormously appreciated: make sure that you are seen as the sort of boss who expects to be asked.

- Remember employees' birthdays, and, without being intrusive, take an interest in their families. Treat them, as far as you possibly can, as friends, while remembering that too close a relationship may make it difficult for you to exercise your business responsibilities.

- Send a postcard to the store when you are away on vacation.

- Make sure that all employees have good equipment to work with, and that they are physically comfortable. The finest cash register will be scorned if it's at an uncomfortable height, and a cashier who is on her feet nearly all day needs a cushioned mat to stand on, and a chair for occasional relaxation. The back-room, too, must be arranged so that new merchandise can be unpacked and checked as comfortably and efficiently as possible. Unpacking a carton on the floor is uncomfortable and tiring: having a knee-high table to put it on makes all the difference.

- Provide a lunch-room where employees can make coffee, eat lunch, and relax. A coffee machine, a sink, a refrigerator, a dish-washer, and a microwave oven do not take up much room, and are deeply appreciated. Be very clear though, about whose responsibility it is to keep it all clean.

- Provide a lockable locker for each employee. Sneak-thieves are possible in even the most respectable neighborhoods, and everyone appreciates having one little piece of lockable privacy.

- Provide a simple first-aid kit, and make sure that everyone knows where it is. Cut fingers and headaches are not uncommon, and it makes life a lot more pleasant if remedies are to hand.

- A profit sharing scheme can be a wonderful incentive. This is dealt with more fully under its own heading.

- Christmas or Annual Bonus, if paid at all, should be in accordance with a fixed and known plan, fully understood by all. It should not come to be taken for granted, or expected as a right, or there will be much ill feeling if it cannot be afforded, or is much reduced, in a bad year.

- Train employees thoroughly not only in standard duties, but also in how to handle unusual situations. A well-trained employee will feel confident and comfortable at work, with resulting good morale. The reverse is true if training has been sketchy or neglected. Training should include instruction on general policy, as well as in specific duties, so that the unexpected can be handled as you would have wished had you been there. This will not only please you, but will also present a valuable image of consistency to the public.

- In most small retail stores, there will be just one boss – owner or manager – so there will be no confusion as to who is in charge, but sometimes an employee may feel entitled to give orders to another, producing the "Please do this" – "But Mary told me to do that" problem, which can be avoided if you set up a clear structure in the first place.

KEY DISCIPLINE: Have as few keys as possible. The fewer people who have keys, the better your security. More about Security under that heading.

KEYSTONE: The trade word for 100% Mark-Up (the same as 50% profit: if retail is $2 and cost is $1, Mark-Up is 100%, but Profit, being half the retail price, is 50%). If you are invoiced for merchandise at s.r.p. (suggested retail price, also called "list") less 50%, the invoice is said to be "at Keystone," but if freight has been charged, s.r.p. will not yield a true 50% Keystone profit. If the invoice is at cost ("net") then for full 50% profit you can "Keystone it" by factoring in the freight. Cost $1, Freight $0.10, TDC (True Delivered Cost) $1.10, retail at Keystone $2.20.

KITCHEN: As mentioned elsewhere, the provision of even the most minimal facilities for coffee breaks and lunches increases efficiency by keeping everyone on the premises, and increases job-satisfaction by providing not only comfort, but somewhere to enjoy a bag lunch from home and save a little money. A small table, microwave, sink and re-frigerator are all that is needed, and do not take much room. Those who use them, however, must keep them clean.

L

LANGUAGE: Much business can be lost if you do not speak your customer's language. Particularly in the states bordering Mexico, Spanish is becoming increasingly widespread, but there is still a tendency to believe that people from south of the border who speak no English must be poor. You will never know unless you speak Spanish, and you may then be surprised at the number of good customers you will gain. If you have any aptitude for it at all, and if there is a substantial foreign speaking population in your area, it is well worth learning the language: it will broaden your customer base. If it is not something you can tackle yourself, consider paying for lessons for some of your staff. They might welcome the opportunity.

LATENESS: In a small store, where everyone is dependent on everyone else, punctuality is important, and an owner-operator should set the example. It is a matter of courtesy to each other, rather than imposed discipline, and if there is a problem, that is the way to approach it. If staff clock in, then lateness will carry its own automatic financial penalty, but it is more effective in the long run to put the emphasis on teamwork and courtesy. *See also* Time Clock.

LAY-AWAY: A Lay-Away plan can yield excellent results if it is well organized and closely monitored. It also needs to be well advertised in the store, because for every customer who asks there will be 99 who don't (and this applies to every moment of retailing. It is astonishing how often a simple "Are you finding what you want?" will lead to a sale, where the customer would otherwise have wandered out without asking – or buying).

The plan should be simple, with written rules as to the amount of the down payment, frequency and amount of subsequent payments, interest charged (if any), and consequences of non-payment. As always, the rules are more to prevent misunderstanding than for their own sake, so you can tailor the plan to suit particular circumstances.

Accurate records are necessary not only for you and the customer, but also because when you take inventory you will need to account for items which have been partly paid for. Check with your accountant for the right way to do this.

LEASE: Your landlord, just like you, is in business to make money by serving customers – tenants – but while your customers can abandon you at will, you and your landlord are tied together by a Lease, and have only one chance to check each other out before committing yourselves to a long-term relationship. You will be asked at least for Financial Statements and perhaps a business plan, plus architect's drawings of your proposed lay-out, and much other information to prove that you are the sort of tenant who will be a credit to the mall or shopping center. The Lease may run to fifty legal-size pages, with clauses ranging from standard penalties for default in rent payment, to detailed specifications of the size, type and color of your store sign. However tedious it may be, read it right through carefully, and if necessary discuss it with the landlord, who may be much more accommodating than the strict legalese of the document might suggest.

If you are in the slightest doubt, have your attorney read it, to make sure that there are no undetected pitfalls.

The Lease specifies all the obligations of your tenancy, and the penalties if you fail to meet them, but make sure that it also specifies the lessor's obligations, and your recourse if he is at fault. Before committing to a lease, do some background checking. Find out how long the lessor has been in business, and who actually owns the premises. Talk to other tenants, and walk round their premises. Be sure that the person you are dealing with is a responsible landlord, and not merely a rent-collector.

Landlord and tenant should, in fact, be virtual partners in a joint enterprise for mutual benefit: good tenants attract customers, creating traffic which increases the rentability of other premises in the center, while good premises and services in turn attract good tenants.

As a very rough classification it can be said that there are three types of landlord: the private owner, with whom you will deal personally; the small corporation, where you will deal with the office, but have access to the boss; and the big corporation, where you will be dealing with responsible representatives or leasing agents.

You can have just as good, or bad, a relationship with the representative of a big corporation as with a private owner, but you will probably find, as in every type of business, that flexibility decreases as the size of the organization increases.

Many leases, particularly in malls, charge either a minimum rent, or a percentage (often 6%) of Gross Sales, whichever is greater. Given that arrangement it is reasonable to assume that the minimum rent will be based on 6% of truly achievable Gross Sales, but consider this cautionary tale: a retailer was offered a location in a new mall, with that rent arrangement. He asked the lessors what Gross Sales per square foot per year he could expect, for his type of store in their type of mall in that location, and was told, in encouraging tones, "at least $150 to $200." In fact, however, the minimum rent amounted to 6% of $470 per square foot, and when this was pointed out, the quote was immediately reduced by 40%.

Nearly all leases now are "triple net": *i.e.* three charges are added to the basic rent – property taxes, insurance, and common area maintenance. There may also be other charges such as advertising and promotion for the mall or center, and perhaps an optional charge for including your store name on the large sign at the entrance. All these extras may add 20% or more to the basic rent, so when making your budget it is prudent to regard the gross sum as rent, regardless of its actual composition.

Remember, but do not take too literally, one experienced tenant's advice on how to assess a lease: "the first thing to find out is how to get out of it."

LEASEHOLD IMPROVEMENTS. Putting in a new floor, or remodeling, or installing a new air conditioner, are Leasehold Improvements for which under a normal lease you will probably have to pay, unless you come to some special agreement with the landlord. You will recover the cost to the extent that it is a tax-deductible Expense in the form of depreciation. Be careful, therefore, not to undertake Leasehold Improvements if the term of your Lease expires before the full maturity of the depreciation period. If you do have to move before a new air conditioner, for instance, is fully depreciated, you can take the balance of depreciation as a lump-sum tax-deductible write-off the next year – but you have to leave the air-conditioner behind!

LIABILITY: The Liabilities of a business are its debts and obligations, and their place in the Accounts is in the Balance Sheet, where they are balanced, with Retained Earnings and Owner's Equity, against the Assets. Your accountant or a text-book will show how they are classified, and there is an example under Balance Sheet, *which see.*

Liability Insurance covers the risks of injury to employees, customers, contractors, or anyone else who may be injured while on the premises, and also protects against general lawsuits. *See* Insurance.

Product Liability – for injury or illness allegedly caused by a product which you have sold – should not normally be a worry, as suit will lie against the manufacturer and distributor, rather than against the innocent retailer (who in any case probably is not regarded as having deep enough pockets to be worth suing). Care should be taken, however, on any items which you may import direct from an overseas source, where you may be the only person available to be sued.

LIGHTING: Just as in display, books have been written on this subject, and careers devoted to it, so this is the place for only a few general suggestions.

Lighting, more than any other single element of store design, can set the mood: bright and cheerful; softly romantic; warm and cozy; flashy art deco; museum dignity – whatever the mood, the lighting will express it. Remember, though, that whatever the mood, the primary purpose of lighting, after basic illumination of the store as a whole, is to flatter the merchandise so that it tempts the customer from every angle. As we mentioned under display, it is no good highlighting the merchandise if the spotlight is frying the customer's head or, from another angle, shining straight into her dazzled eyes.

Most stores will find that the best results are obtained with a combination of fluorescent and incandescent. Fluorescent lights are the coolest and most economical, and will provide the basic store-wide illumination, but for accenting the merchandise some incandescents are needed, and the most effective way to use them is in track. This gives maximum flexibility in positioning, and also in type of light; spot or flood, high or low wattage, high-intensity halogen, or regular incandescent, plus color.

When installing fluorescent, be aware of the various types of light that are available. Some tubes, for instance, will give a gentle, almost cream colored illumination, others a stark operating-room white, and many other tones are available. This is one of the critical choices in establishing the mood you are after.

Timers can be very useful. The window display lights, for instance, may not be needed at all until evening, particularly if the day is sunny, and a timer to switch them on automatically in the late afternoon, and off again when you have closed, prolongs bulb life and saves energy (on dark and stormy days, you can manually override the timer). Prolonging bulb life can be surprisingly important, not only in saving money, but also in saving a great deal of trouble, because bulb-replacement often requires a lot of display moving and ladder climbing.

If you have outside lighting, of course, a timer is essential, as you almost certainly do not want it on during the day, and you do not want to have to remember it every evening. Also, you may well want it to remain on for a while after you have closed, but not all night, so you can set it to turn on at dusk, and off again at, perhaps, 10 p.m.

Remember to re-set timers with the seasons, and for daylight saving time.

LOAN: A loan will presumably be needed once, to get a new business started, and then perhaps annually, as a Bridging Loan, to finance purchases of Christmas inventory. The starting loan will always be the hardest to get, but totally impossible without a well-presented Business Plan (*which see*). Bridging Loans for an established business can be almost routine provided your financial statement is sound. All barriers fall, of course, if you have solid collateral outside the business, and are ready to stake it on your success. Some banks were prepared to take some small risks in the past, but nowadays they will only lend on a virtual guarantee that they will get their money back: they are not interested in risk, or persuaded by optimism.

You cannot calculate how much you will need to borrow, nor will the Bank be eager to lend, without a Budget, showing monthly Cash Flow and Cash Need. This will ensure that you borrow the absolute minimum necessary and will also give you the information to plan a schedule for drawing from a Line of Credit, paying interest only on what you have drawn, rather than borrowing all at once.

If your financial year ends on 31st December, and you apply for a loan the following September, you may be asked for a recent Financial Statement, which cannot be completed without a figure for Inventory. If you are fully computerized, this presents no problem (*see* Computers), but otherwise you will have to take physical inventory again, or calculate it by taking starting inventory (from your last year-end Financial Statement), plus purchases to date, less sales to date. This presents no difficulty, but it does require that your bookkeeping is sufficiently well organized and well kept that purchases and sales data are easily isolated and retrieved. *See* Financing a Business.

LOCATION. The right location depends on the type of store, but the following general guide-lines may help in making the choice:

- Your store should be among others of similar quality, but not directly competitive, both for the obvious reason, and because some vendors will not open a new account close to an existing one.
- If considering a mall or major shopping center, check out the anchor store.
    - Is it an up-market department store or...
    - a discount house? Which would suit you?

In any case there should be a prosperous and busy atmosphere, with plenty of foot traffic. Note that nearly all stores will be branches of regional or national chains, and it will be hard to find any that are owner-operated. If you are thinking of opening in such a location, be very sure of your business plan and your research. The economics of such a location are more suitable for corporate investment and manager-operated branches than for individual ventures.

When considering any location, ask the landlord for all the demographic information he can give you. Any major lessor of mall or shopping center premises will have a fat brochure with informative maps, charts, and tabulated data. This will be helpful, but will only include, of course, the favorable aspects.

You will probably be opening in your home town, but even so do not take your local knowledge for granted. Check out all the shopping centers and malls which you do not usually go to, and spend time exploring the city as if you were a stranger, not forgetting the stranger's obvious first resource, the Chamber of Commerce.

Do not be afraid to ask retailers in a potential location for any information they can give you about the landlord, the level of activity compared to previous years, changes in the neighborhood, the crime rate, and any other points that you may consider relevant.

Possibly the most important single factor in considering premises, other things being equal, is the quality of the parking. However attractive your store, if customers find parking difficult they will not come – certainly not as often or in such numbers as they would otherwise. Any modern mall or shopping center, of course, should have adequate and convenient parking, but check out the details. If you are considering opening a gift shop next to a popular restaurant, for instance, your store-front parking will probably be pre-empted by the restaurant's lunch customers from about 11 to 2.

Consider whether the direction in which the store windows face is going to be important. In the Southern states, for instance, south facing windows will add to the air-conditioning bill, and window displays will be limited to items which will not fade or suffer from heat (unless you have tinted glass, which has disadvantages – *see* Display).

Some of your merchandise will probably arrive in big 18-wheeler trailer rigs. Make sure that there is adequate access.

Rents in a shopping center or mall will vary depending on the site. There are very good reasons for this, and you may well find, in comparing a low-rent and a high-rent site, that the higher traffic in the high-rent site will generate sales more than offsetting the extra rent.

If considering premises in a new center under construction, you will see a bare carcass, lacking sheet-rock on the walls, a ceiling, lighting and other essentials. The cost of providing these will theoretically be covered by the landlord's offer of a "build-out allowance," which will be in dollars per square foot. Usually this will be enough for no more than a plain vanilla empty box, with bare concrete floor, standard drop ceiling with fluorescent panels, and the standard shop front. It is not uncommon for tenants to spend as much again as the build-out allowance on design and display, apart from the cost of opening inventory.

LOCKERS: Lockable lockers should be provided for all staff. Not only do they provide security against sneak-thieves (and to protect yourself, employees should be specifically told to use them), it is also good for morale, in showing thoughtfulness, and providing a small measure of privacy.

LOGO: The Logo plays a vital part in creating something very important; a consistent, recognizable and memorable Image for your store (*see* Advertising). Big companies spend millions of dollars on the design of logos, including the daunting task of making them suitable for use on everything from business cards to water towers and trucks, and even for your small business the logo must be adaptable to stationery, business cards, custom labels, print advertising, and perhaps custom packaging. Some logos are absolutely beautiful, but say nothing. Make sure that yours provides a graphic clue to the nature of your business, and that it conveys, by the quality of design, the store Image which you are aiming at.

LOLLIPOPS: The idea is fast fading that the ideal treat for a child is a lollipop. Dental health is regarded as far more important now than it used to be (apart from being very expensive), and mothers can be quite offended if Little Willie appears sucking a lollipop. If you extend your public relations to the young, remember that the lasting impact will be on the parents. Balloons with your store name on them, for instance, will keep everyone happy.

Music

M

MAIL: If you are in hospital the first thing the nurse does every day is take your pulse, regardless of what is the matter with you. However healthy your business may be, always treat it like a delicate patient: by opening the mail every day you will be keeping your finger on its pulse, and gain an insight into its state of health which you can obtain in no other way. You will miss no opportunities, and problems will be nipped in the bud.

Letters from customers, of course, must be dealt with first, then Invoices, to keep you abreast of what merchandise is coming in, to check the costing, and also to ensure that no discounts, freight allowances, insurance claims, or mis-charges are missed; then anything else financial, to ensure that there are no problems such as vendor complaints of late payment (payments should neither be late nor, and almost as important, early; if you have 30 days, take thirty days, and have the money working for you in the meantime). You will also see the state and federal tax forms: unwelcome but perhaps useful reminders.

With all that taken care of, you can enjoy the vendors' catalogs, the quote for your new sign, the copy of the Purchase Order from the representative you saw the other day, the invitation to the Small Business Management Seminar (only $750 for six hours), and all the other fascinating literature which lands in a retailer's mail box every day. But deal with it today – left unattended it will start to engulf your desk like a lava flow – and don't leave anything unopened just because you think you know what is in it: this can lead to nasty surprises.

It is important to delegate, but opening the mail is one chore that you should keep to yourself: what you delegate is the action dictated by the contents.

MAIL ORDER: There are three grades of mail order business:

- Accept and ship mail and telephone orders without issuing a catalog or price list. This is well worth the trouble, and builds up a surprising amount of business, not to mention goodwill. You should anyway be ready to ship gifts for in-store customers, and the recipients may order from you themselves.

- Make a simple catalog or price-list of what the store normally carries in stock, or a selection. Have it as a hand-out in the store, send it to the mailing list generated from your customers, and take inexpensive advertising to announce its availability, so that people can send for it. This sort of price-list can readily be produced on your computer.

- Produce a full-scale mail order catalog, buy a mailing list to extend the customer base to people who have never heard of the store, and go fully into the mail order business. This is a major undertaking. It should be treated as a separate enterprise, and is not within the scope of this book.

MAINTENANCE: The Lease will specify what is your responsibility, and what is the landlord's. You do not want to pay for something that is not your problem, nor do you want needlessly to antagonize the landlord by demanding that he pay for something that is not his.

If, for instance, the store needs a new floor, is it the landlord's responsibility, or will you have to pay for it as a Leasehold Improvement? The answer will depend on the Lease, on how long you have been a tenant, and perhaps on your personal relations with the landlord. In many cases friendly negotiations can modify the letter of the law.

The air conditioner can be a major maintenance expense, and when signing a new lease it is wise to check on its age and condition, and on the exact terms concerning maintenance and replacement.

Do not wait for something to go wrong or wear out before finding out who should repair it. If it is up to the landlord, he will not know unless you tell him, and if it is up to you, it can be dealt with quickly. It can be costly to leave a job undone just because there is uncertainty about who should do it.

MANAGER: Whether you simply need someone to stand in for when you are away on vacation or a buying trip, or whether you are an absentee owner, give your manager a full and detailed job description, including the scope and limitations of responsibilities, and clear achievement goals. Whatever the owner-manager relationship, it can be damaged by your neglect or by your interference. Make a job description for yourself, which will ensure that you avoid both extremes, and at the same time will keep you fully informed and in control. *See* Delegating Authority.

MANUFACTURER: Whenever possible, deal directly with the manufacturer. You may order through a Broker, but you will still be invoiced by the manufacturer, and the relationship remains direct. This is not always possible with foreign manufacturers, but *see* Importing.

In some types of business, such as foodstuffs and hardware, the trade structure may be keyed entirely to wholesale distribution, but as this makes a level playing field for all, there is no problem. Where there is an alternative, it is obviously advantageous to deal with the manufacturer rather than a middleman, not only because of the better price, but because the middleman may not carry the whole of the manufacturer's range. The middleman does have two advantages to offset his higher prices: he may accept smaller orders, and he may have stock of an item while the manufacturer is between production runs. *See* Distributor.

MARGIN, MARK-UP, MARK-DOWN. *See* Costing and Profit Margin.

MINIMUM ORDER: There are three Minimum Order requirements. First, a vendor may require a quite large minimum for a first order, so that his product will be adequately displayed both in quantity and diversity. Secondly, there is the very much lower re-order minimum, which rarely presents a problem, and thirdly, there is the minimum required for the vendor to pay the freight. This may present a problem, as it can be as high, in the specialty food trade for instance, as $1,750 or 500 pounds weight. Always make sure, when ordering, that you know the minimum order requirement, even when ordering personally from sales reps, who have been known to forget about it, and you find yourself paying freight when you did not want to.

MIRRORS: When designing the store, look for opportunities to use mirrors. They make almost any premises look larger and lighter, and can be particularly effective behind the type of shelving which is on brackets slotted into metal standards.

MOTIVATION: Do some severe self-analysis before deciding to run your own show. The small retailer is an entrepreneur – an independent business man – with all the responsibility and anxiety that that entails, and you must be sure that that is the way of life which you want and in which you can succeed.

Do not assume that success, even brilliance, in a previous career will qualify you to run a business. The qualification you need is not business success, but the ability and desire to be independent.

The most important factors are knowledge, self-discipline, enthusiasm, the ability to motivate other people (both your staff and your customers!), perseverance, and humility. Humility may surprise you, but learning is endless. One of Deming's great principles was the necessity of a conscious policy of continuous improvement, and on a lighter note, the winner of the Master's one year at Augusta – a man at the very peak of his profession – attributed part of his success to the advice of his caddie.

Above all, be clear about your goals. Why do you want to own a retail store? Do you want to build it up into an empire, sell it, and retire early to Hawaii? Do you feel it is the most satisfying way of preparing for a financially secure old age? Is it simply the best investment for your money? Do you have a particularly keen interest in the type of merchandise you aim to carry? The nature of the goal is not important, provided it is real. One totally invalid reason for wanting to own a retail store is that you think it will be "fun." Those who say this base it on what they have seen as customers: they have no inkling of, or interest in, what goes on behind the "employees only" door.

The real pleasure of being your own master is that you never have to explain your decisions to anyone. *This, however, means that you must always explain them very clearly to yourself.*

MUSIC: Farmers have found that music in the milking shed causes the cows to give more milk. Music in the store may likewise make the customers give more money (but it should not be too loud). Select it with your customers' tastes in mind, not your own (unless you are sure they coincide). The sales-defeating atmosphere of a dead silent store on a rainy day with two customers whispering as if at a funeral has to be felt to be believed.

N – P

NET INCOME: Do not be deceived: this is not all money in the bank. For one thing, capital expenditure on such things as copiers, computers, or display fixtures, does not show up on the Net Income Statement at all. Some of it will, as Depreciation, which is an Expense, but not the rest. The Net Income Statement is simply a report card on your operating performance – Sales, Cost of the Goods Sold, and running Expenses, or overhead.

Even then, the so-called Net Income is not all money. Some of it will be in the value of your Inventory. This is because the value of the goods which you have sold is, quite logically, the value of Inventory at the end of the year, subtracted from the purchases made during the year, plus the inventory at the beginning.

A	**Gross Sales**	90,000	90,000
	Opening Inventory	100,000	100,000
	Plus Purchases	50,000	50,000
	Less Closing Inventory	100,000	125,000
B	***Cost of Goods Sold***	***50,000***	***25,000***
	GROSS PROFIT (A – B)	40,000	75,000
	Less Expenses	35,000	35,000
	NET INCOME	5,000	40,000

Obviously, in the left column, we've sold what we bought, no more, no less. But if Closing Inventory were $125,000 (right column), Cost of Goods Sold would be only $25,000, and the Net Income would go up by exactly the same amount. Sales, however, are the same. In the first instance, the cost of the goods sold was 55.56% of Sales, which is achievable. In the second instance, the figures suggest that $25,000 worth of goods were sold for $90,000, a cost of goods sold of 27.78%, which is nonsense. The money is not in the bank. It is in the stock room.

NET SALES: The actual amount of money earned by sales, less any returns, discounts, etc. It may appear on the Income Statement as Gross, or merely Sales, because the total entered from the cash register's daily printout will have taken such adjustments into account, and there will be no further deductions to be made.

The distinction between Gross Sales and Net Sales, although real, is in fact no longer of any significance, now that cash registers calculate the Net figure for you. *See* Gross Sales.

Net Sales

NEWSLETTER: This can be a profitable sales tool if you have a good mailing list of loyal customers, if you have something to say, if you have the time and the will to keep it going, and if production and distribution costs are not too high.

Production costs can be very low if you have a good computer, but postal rates are now high enough to be critical, and other means of distribution may be more economical, such as door-to-door delivery, or as an insert in the type of small local weekly newspaper that is distributed free.

A computer/cash register will keep a classified list of customers, based on what they have bought, how often, and for how much. This enables you to prepare specialized newsletters aimed at particular targets, which is obviously the most cost-effective method of using them.

A Newsletter must be either regular – weekly, monthly, or quarterly – or scheduled for sales peaks such as Valentine's, Mother's Day, etc. If its issue is random, you will lack the necessary discipline of a deadline, and may let it slide to oblivion, and even if you do get out a late issue the long absence may make customers wonder about the store's well-being.

Do not commit to a Newsletter unless you are confident that you will have something interesting to say for several future issues, and that it will repay its cost in increased sales.

NO ANTICIPATION: This term appears on some Invoices, as, for instance "Terms: Net 30. No anticipation." This means that you cannot unilaterally take a discount for earlier payment.

OPEN TO BUY: This is a technical phrase used by large retailers and refers to the amount of money available for purchasing in a given period. It is arrived at by a formula based on Gross Sales, cost of goods sold, and any other factors which management may choose to use, depending on net profit and growth projections. The simplest formula would be Gross Sales $100,000, Cost of Goods Sold $55,000, Open to Buy $55,000; but this merely replaces what has been sold, and is Subsistence Retailing, which leads to stagnation, decline, and failure. A useful Open To Buy figure must be based not only on Cost of Goods Sold, but also on Sales Analysis, Net Income, and projected growth, so that the new purchasing will take into account not only replacement of what has sold, but also the dropping of slow-selling lines, the increase of fast-selling lines, and an overall increase in quantity or value over and above Cost of Goods Sold, which will be paid for out of Net Income, to an extent to be determined by projected, or planned, Growth. This means, of course, that you cannot arrive at an Open To Buy figure unless you have reliable Sales Analysis, monthly Income Statements, and budgeted Growth projections.

OPENING HOURS: *See* Hours of Business.

ORDER NUMBER: *see* Purchase Order.

OVERHEAD. All operating expenses after you have paid for the goods that have been sold. It is not a technical Accounting term, and in the Income Statement it is shown as Expenses.

OVERTIME: If you employ hourly paid staff, it is wise, when first hiring, to specify overtime rates if you expect to be asking them for extra work during the Christmas season or for taking inventory. This makes for a much better relationship than asking for favors which they may find annoying to grant, but embarrassing to refuse.

PACKING LIST: Also called a Packing Slip, and sometimes Picking Slip. It lists what should be in the carton, or in a whole multi-carton shipment, and may or may not show prices. It should be checked against the Purchase Order and the Invoice, and will be needed if there is any discrepancy. It is not an accounting document of record, and need not be kept if the shipment is complete and undamaged, unless you wish to staple it to the Purchase Order.

PAINTING: It is astonishing how quickly and effectively you can change the look of a store with a roller and a paint-pot. If the store needs a face-lift, it may well be possible to do all that is necessary by these simple means, without having recourse to expensive remodeling or the purchase of new fixtures. When faced with a problem, consider the simple and inexpensive solution first.

PARKING: As mentioned under location, one of the most critical features of a store is its parking lot. It should of course have plenty of room, and easy access, but above all it should be reserved for customers. The owner who parks in front of his own store, or who allows his employees to do so, is sabotaging his business. If the average parking time is thirty minutes, and the average sale as little as $7.50, the yield per parking space per nine-hour day is $135, which translates into $48,600 in a 360 day year. These figures are arbitrary, but adequate to show the importance of parking spaces, and that as owner you should park somewhere else, and make sure your employees do likewise.

PARTNERSHIP: This is probably the most risky business structure, because it injects money into what was probably an existing social or family relationship. This is not to say that partnership cannot succeed, but to do so, whether the partners are old friends or strangers, it must be based on a very clear and detailed Partnership Agreement, laying out exactly the roles and responsibilities of each partner and the method, amount and timing of each partner's remuneration. The Agreement must also lay down procedures for settling disputes, perhaps with provision for an arbitrator (including the method of his selection), so that in the event of disagreement the partners can refer to the rule book rather than argue each other out of business, and perhaps out of friendship.

PART TIMERS: Do not confuse part-time with temporary or cut-rate. For the retail trade, the best help may be found among those who do not need to, or who cannot, work full time. This does not mean that they cannot become permanent. Some of the best salespeople I have known have been housewives who have worked four or five hours a day, and who have done so for periods of years. Looking for such help not only gives you access to a great many highly qualified people (they are usually discerning shoppers themselves), but has the additional advantage that their part-time presence minimizes the difficulty if they are absent. So far as is possible they should have all the benefits of full-timers, and their pay scale should be equivalent.

P. O. NUMBER. Purchase Order Number. *See* Purchase Order.

PERMITS. Check with City Hall about Permits. There will be special permits if you handle any foods, tobacco or liquor, perhaps one for any free-standing sign which you may have. Extensive re-modeling, too, may need a building permit, but this is your concern only if you do it independently (with, of course, landlord's consent). If the landlord does it for you, it is up to him to get the permit.

PERSONNEL. Keep full personnel records, preferably on standard forms obtainable from office supply houses. It is worth it for only one employee, so that you have a record of deductions claimed, salaries and wages paid, etc., all in one place, complete with date of hiring, home address, telephone number and Social Security Number, plus a history of any problems and how they were resolved (and keep a form for yourself: you may want to check a salary change or payment date). Employee Leasing (*which see*) will take care of all this for you, including the provision of counseling if needed, but the basic record sheet, with original application form (if any), should also be in your own file. *See also* Job Satisfaction.

PETTY CASH: Petty Cash is not petty. If it is not properly accounted for it will leak cash like a dripping tap, and if you are audited there may be questions about where the money went.

There are two ways of accounting for Petty Cash. The traditional way is to keep a Petty Cash Account, with the actual cash and the receipts in a cash box, separate from the cash register. To open the Petty Cash Account, write a check on the Checking Account – say $100 – and put the cash in the Petty Cash box. Bookkeeping will show this as a Credit (yes, that's right) in the Checking Account, and a Debit in the Petty Cash Account. At the end of the month, take the receipts for the month's purchases from the cash box. Say they are $25.50 for Office Supplies, and $13.00 for Postage: the Office Supplies account and the Postage account will be Debited these amounts, and the Petty Cash account Credited with the total of $38.50. Actual cash remaining in the box should be $61.50, and a replenishment check for $38.50 will bring it back up to the original $100: the check will show as a credit in the Checking account, and the cash as a Debit in Petty Cash.

It seems odd to record a check drawn on the checking account as a Credit, but it becomes clear if you imagine that you are the checking account yourself: if a check has been written, and money has gone out, then you, as the checking account, are owed the amount that has gone – it is a debt in your favor, so it is a Credit. Double entry bookkeeping becomes much easier to follow if you apply this idea throughout.

Accounting for Petty Cash:	Debit	Credit	
To open the account: a Check		100.00	*Checking acct.*
Cash into box	100.00		*Petty Cash acct.*
Spent from box: Office	25.50		*Office supplies acct.*
Postage	13.00		*Postage acct.*
Total expenditure		38.50	*Petty Cash acct.*
Replenish cash in box: a Check		38.50	*Checking acct.*
Cash into box	38.50		*Petty Cash acct.*
Showing that all accts balance	177.00	177.00	

If your bookkeeping is on computer, you can do away with the separate Petty Cash system, and make petty cash purchases straight out of the register, because the daily Cash Reconciliation can be done by entry in the General Journal. Total recorded Sales are entered in the Credit Column, balanced in the Debit column by the Bank Deposit, Credit Card Sales and any expenditures. Every entry will be by account number, so for instance $7.50 to the window cleaner (whose receipt will be in the register) will be entered against the account number for Repairs and Maintenance. This does away with the need for a separate cash box and Petty Cash account, as every expenditure is posted to the correct account the same day.

PHANTOM PROFIT: it is possible to be forced out of business for lack of cash even though the Net Income Statement shows a profit, because that profit – the "Net Income" – is not by any means all cash. In the following exaggerated example there is apparently a fabulous Net Income of $180,000, but Closing Inventory is worth $252,000. In other words, the "profit" is, in the familiar phrase "tied up in Inventory," rather than being cash in the bank.

A	SALES		360,000	
	Opening Inventory	90,000		
	Plus Purchases	+180,000		
B	Total Opening Inv. + Purchases	270,000		
C	Less Closing Inventory	−252,000		
D	COST OF GOODS SOLD (B–C)	18,000	18,000	5.00%
	Gross Profit (A–D)		342,000	95.00%
	Minus EXPENSES		−162,000	−45.00%
	NET INCOME		180,000	50.00%

Such figures are obviously impossible – you are not going to sell $18,000 worth of goods for $360,000 – they simply demonstrate how excess inventory produces phantom Net Income. The next example shows a more normal situation, with an ideal 50% Gross Profit, and a realistic Net Income.

A	SALES		360,000	
	Opening Inventory	90,000		
	Plus Purchases	+180,000		
B	Total Opening Inv. + Purchases	270,000		
C	Less Closing Inventory	−90,000		
D	COST OF GOODS SOLD (B–C)	180,000	180,000	50.00%
	Gross Profit (A–D)		180,000	50.00%
	Minus EXPENSES		−162,000	−45.00%
	NET INCOME		18,000	5.00%

The following example, however, shows the result of living off your fat – too drastic reduction of Inventory:

A	**SALES**		**360,000**	
	Opening Inventory	90,000		
	Plus Purchases	180,000		
B	**Total Opening Inv. + Purchases**	**270,000**		
C	**Less Closing Inventory**	**70,000**		
D	**COST OF GOODS SOLD (B–C)**	**200,000**	**200,000**	**55.56%**
	Gross Profit (A–D)		160,000	44.44%
	Minus EXPENSES		162,000	45.00%
	NET INCOME		**–2,000**	**–0.56%**

Out of $270,000 worth of opening inventory and purchases, only $70,000 worth is left – $200,000 worth have been sold for $360,000 worth of sales, resulting in a meager Gross Profit that does not even cover Expenses – a net loss of $2,000.

In other words, for most small retailers, Net Income is a theoretical figure which reflects a combination of cash in the bank and the portion of closing inventory paid for but not yet sold. Nor does it take into account the deferred expense of outstanding Depreciation on furniture, fixtures and equipment. If you buy a $10,000 piece of equipment depreciable over five years, in its first year only $2,000 of Depreciation will appear as an Expense on the Income Statement. The other $8,000 will be on the Balance Sheet as an Asset. The money has been spent, but its absence is not reflected in the figure of Net Income, which must be understood as a performance rating, not a bank statement (and will anyway not be ready, unless you have a fully integrated computer system, for some weeks after the end of the financial year).

With cash tied up in inventory and other assets, you may find yourself having to sell the assets to pay the bills, and this can mean going out of business. Even when cash is tied up in good saleable inventory, that inventory will only sell and become cash at a certain speed, which may not be fast enough. To speed up sales, profit margins will have to be cut, gross profit will decline, and you are still in trouble (which is the scenario in the third example above). You can, of course, try to borrow from the bank, with the assets as collateral, but the interest is expensive, and the loan still has to be repaid – in cash.

Inventory Control and the Cash Flow Forecast (*which see*) are the tools which will prevent these problems from arising. They are indeed the only way to ensure that Purchasing is in step with Sales, and that cash is used to best advantage, with all commitments and budget plans met, and remedial action taken if there is a shortage.

PHILOSOPHY: There are two extremes in the behavior of new store owners. At one extreme are those who treat the enterprise more or less as an amateur hobby. They buy some attractive fixtures, and a few shelves for the stock room, and believe that there is no more to it than just buying the merchandise, being nice to customers, and paying the bills once a month (probably writing the checks by hand on the kitchen table at home). At the other extreme are those who regard ownership of a business as equivalent to being CEO of a Fortune 500 company. They employ an expensive store design consultant, buy fixtures which would catch the eye in Tiffany's or Nieman Marcus, install a computer system to match, equip the office with fitted carpet, mahogany desks, and real leather executive chairs, and retain expensive attorneys, and accountants.

In between are the successful retailers who use this *Owner's Manual*. They understand that capital is a finite resource (small retail stores are notoriously under-capitalized), that the showroom, whether lavish or simple, must complement the merchandise and attract the customers, and that the office and stock room are work areas which need only sturdy, practical equipment.

They understand, too, that a store is neither hobby nor empire, but a business requiring professional management, and that retailing is a trade, to be learned like any other.

Customers expect professional service; vendors, bankers, and tax authorities expect professional conduct. To succeed and prosper, the store owner must be a fully professional retailer. *See* Professionalism.

PLANNING: Survival in retailing depends upon growth – increasing Net Income – and you cannot increase Net Income without a plan, so Planning becomes one of the most important functions of ownership (*see* Time Management). It involves all aspects of the business from making out vacation schedules (which may not increase Net Income, but can certainly prevent decrease) to deciding on a move to larger premises or a renewal of the Lease.

Planning requires tools, from the simple – a whole-year wall calendar – to the complex – such as a current Income Statement, Cash Flow Forecast, Budget, and, of course, the check register reconciled to date, showing cash on hand.

It cannot be emphasized too strongly that owner-operated retailing (indeed any owner-operated small business) is a seamless operation. The figure of Accounts Payable will affect Purchasing; Cash Flow Forecast will affect Advertising; the Budget will affect decisions on new display units; nearby real estate development will affect foot traffic to the store, and so on and so on, with all these factors affecting each other.

The owner who does not take all these factors into account, and make positive plans for the future, is on a par with the man who was heard to say, as he fell past the thirtieth floor of the Empire State Building, "so far, so good."

Note that nothing has been said about Tax Returns. All planning must take account of the tax burden, and aim to minimize it, but the tax returns themselves are by-products. It is fatal to treat bookkeeping and accounting as merely necessary evils to satisfy the IRS. They are the basic tools of management, without which Planning is impossible, and without Planning there can be no Growth.

PRICING GUNS: Nothing loses a sale quicker than a piece which is not priced. No customer should ever have to ask for a price (although many will, for fear of handling a delicate piece, or because they are not wearing their spectacles), and a good pricing gun is essential. The price-tag should have two lines; the upper one for a code of your choice, and the lower for the price. The code may show the cost, or the month of purchase, or the department to which the piece belongs, or a combination of these, whichever suits your own management method best. It creates a good impression, too, to have the name of the store on the tag.

The Yellow Pages will list several suppliers of pricing guns, with various choices of label size and numeric or alphabetical output. Generally speaking, the smaller the tag the better, provided there is room for the two lines and the store name, because there is often not room on small items for a large tag.

An important factor in the choice is the ready availability of labels. The ideal is to find the right gun and its labels available in your own city. Sometimes, however, labels for the right gun have to be ordered from afar with a ten-day delivery time. Avoid this if possible. Running out of labels can cause serious problems.

Labels are available in peel-off or hard adhesive, and perforated so that they come apart when being removed. For a gift shop, the peel-off is obviously preferable, unless there is a security problem with thieves swapping labels.

Lastly, chose a gun which can be reloaded easily, so that everyone in the store can do it without asking for help.

PRINTER: There will be receipt printers on the Cash Register and the Credit Card Terminal as part of the hardware, but the office will need a full document printer, and the choices are Dot Matrix, Ink Jet and Laser. The ink jet produces excellent results, and has become so inexpensive that there is hardly any need to consider a dot matrix, especially as the standard cut sheet feed on ink jets makes it so easy to load whatever stationery may be needed, such as checks or letterhead. For all normal purposes, too, modern ink jet print quality is so good that a Laser printer can be considered a luxury. At high volumes, however, the speed and lower operating cost of a Laser printer may well make it the best for your needs.

PRODUCTIVITY: *see* Efficiency.

PROFESSIONALISM: The amateur works to please himself: the professional works to please others. The entrepreneur cannot be an amateur: he is not working to please himself, but to please his customers, his staff, his vendors, his partners, his stockholders, his bank, and the Internal Revenue Service. It is a common misconception that long service as a retail customer fits you for retail management. This is like saying that thousands of hours as an airline passenger fits you to be a pilot. From salesmanship to housekeeping, every aspect of retail management needs skill which must be learned, and much of that skill is applied only behind the "Employees Only" door.

It is a common and very dangerous assumption that because a business is very small it can be run like an amateur hobby, and this is why bad record-keeping is the cause of most small business failures, and general bad management the cause of the rest. The only amateurs you will deal with will be customers: everyone else, particularly the IRS, your bank, and your vendors, will be professionals. Learn your trade, so that you can deal with them on equal terms, in an atmosphere of mutual respect.

Apart from its beneficial effect on all business relationships, professionalism will also free you of much drudgery, which might otherwise make you disenchanted with running your own business. Professional techniques, after all, are the result of the business man's eternal quest to save time, and thus money. If you are happy with long hours at home trying to muddle through an overdue payroll tax return, well and good. If you would prefer to put the completed return in the mail on the way home, and go out to dinner with a clear conscience, take time to learn beforehand what records are needed, how to keep them, where to keep them so that you can lay your hands on them without searching, and how to fill in the form – the professional approach.

The well-trained and well-informed professional inspires confidence. In retailing, to gain the confidence of your customers, your vendors, your staff, your colleagues, your bank, and the IRS is to place yourself well on the road to success.

PROFIT: This word is very loosely used. It can refer to Net Profit, Gross Profit, Profit Before Taxes, Operating Profit, or Profit Margin. It can also refer to profit on individual items, or to the profit of the business over a period of time. What used to be called the Profit and Loss statement is now more commonly called the Net Income Statement, and the Profit on the bottom line is called Net Income. All these forms of Profit are discussed under their own headings, and it is important to be sure of the context when using them. *See also* Phantom Profit.

PROFIT and LOSS ACCOUNT: *see* Income Statement.

PROFIT MARGIN: Sometimes just "Profit" and sometimes just "Margin." As mentioned before, be sure of the context. Margin may refer to Gross Margin, which is Gross Profit expressed as a percentage of Sales (Sales $100,000; Cost of Goods Sold $55,000; Gross Profit $45,000; Gross Margin 45%), or it may refer to the Profit Margin on a single item. If you buy a widget for $1 and retail it for $2, the Margin is 50%, because the Profit is half the retail price. Sometimes, however, this transaction will wrongly be described as having 100% profit, because the retail price is double the cost price.

PROFIT SHARING: There are few more powerful incentives than a share in the profits, but those sharing must have some influence on whether or not a profit is made. Salespeople can increase sales, but only management can influence profit. Incentives for salespeople, therefore, are better based on the direct results of their performance, such as rate of sales per hour.

If Profit Sharing is adopted, and if it is to be effective, the profit to be shared must be clearly defined (*e.g.* Net Income Before Taxes), with an agreement in writing. This must also show the share proportions, plus the method of payment, which may be affected by the recipients' personal tax situation, and by that of the business.

It is wise, therefore, for both the business and the individuals concerned, to take professional advice when setting up a plan. *See* Incentives.

PROJECTIONS: Projections can be dangerous. The one below shows a wonderful profit of $115,000. Let's assume that Sales of $500,000 is a reasonable forecast in view of past performance. Opening Inventory is known. Purchases are based on past performance and on plans to carry some new lines seen at the trade show. The increase in Closing Inventory is estimated as reasonable considering the increase in Purchases – it's all wonderful merchandise and it'll be nice to have it in stock. All quite plausible.

A	Gross Sales	500,000	
	Opening Inventory	125,000	
	Plus Purchases	235,000	
	Less Closing Inventory	200,000	
	Cost of Goods Sold	160,000	
B	GROSS PROFIT (A–B)	340,000	
	Less Expenses	225,000	
	NET INCOME (Loss)	115,000	

Wrong! Wrong! Wrong!

Look at the same chart with percentages added:

A	Gross Sales	500,000	
	Opening Inventory	125,000	25%
	Plus Purchases	235,000	47%
	Less Closing Inventory	200,000	40%
B	**Cost of Goods Sold**	**160,000**	**32%**
	GROSS PROFIT (A–B)	340,000	68%
	Less Expenses	225,000	45%
	NET INCOME (Loss)	115,000	23%

If indeed Sales did not change, each sale would be costing you only 32 cents on the dollar. This is unlikely, to say the least. The $115,000 Net Income would not be money in the bank. The money would actually, in the familiar phrase which I have used elsewhere, be tied up in inventory, *but you would pay income tax on all of it.*

Now look what happens when you reduce that Closing Inventory from $200,000 to $110,000. Cost of Goods Sold becomes a realistic 50%, and more of the Net Income will in the bank rather than the stock room.

A	Gross Sales	500,000	
	Opening Inventory	125,000	25%
	Plus Purchases	235,000	47%
B	Total open. inv. + purchases	360,000	72%
	Less Closing Inventory	110,000	22%
C	**Cost of Goods Sold**	**250,000**	**50%**
	GROSS PROFIT (A–C)	250,000	50%
	Less Expenses	225,000	45%
	NET INCOME (Loss)	115,000	23%

So when you make Projections, always build in the percentages. The bottom line may look the same, but Inventory Control takes money out of the stock room and into the bank.

PROPRIETOR: The sole owner of a private business is usually referred to as the proprietor, and the business structure as a proprietorship. The owner of a corporation is referred to as owner, rather than proprietor.

PUNCTUALITY: *see* Lateness.

PURCHASE ORDERS: It is essential to use serially numbered order forms. The only way to keep accurate track of what has been invoiced against which Purchase Order is to give every order a number, and to make sure that the vendor quotes it on his invoice.

Every Purchase Order must be allocated a number. If a rep writes an order on his own form, make sure it bears your P.O. Number, and attach the P.O. form itself to your copy of the order. It need only have on it the vendor's (not the broker's) name, and "per order form attached," but if your standard form fronts all Purchase Orders, filing and retrieval will be much quicker and easier. Mis-filing and loss are only too likely with the amazing variety of vendors' and brokers' own forms, on which it may be difficult to find your P.O. Number or, on a broker's form, even the vendor's name.

Standard numbered forms printed with your store name and address are readily available from mail order office supply companies. Get some extra unnumbered forms for continuation sheets. Duplicate is enough: one copy for the alphabetical vendor file, and one for a master file in numerical order, as a guard against loss. A rep writing on his own form does not need or want a copy of yours, only the number, and it is no longer necessary to send vendors copies of orders which you have written yourself, as it is now standard practice to fax them.

Although most business software has a Purchase Order menu, it is usually impossible to generate a Purchase Order from it unless the item to be ordered is already in the computer. This requires the allocation of an SKU (Stock Keeping Unit) number to every item of inventory, with description and price, and so much time and effort devoted to data entry that it is probably neither desirable nor necessary in a single small retail store. In any case so many orders are handwritten by reps, or by you in the showroom while checking what is needed, or at a trade show, that the computer becomes irrelevant, as there would be no advantage in re-writing orders into it.

When writing a Purchase Order, do not forget to include a cross-reference to relevant Call Cards and Special Orders (*which see*), and conversely, write the P.O. Number on those.

PURCHASING (or Buying, but the form is always called a Purchase Order): Buying your opening inventory will be limited by the money available, and guided by your research and your taste. It will also, however, be the last time you will have such freedom of choice. All future buying will be partially disciplined by the sales records of the merchandise.

You will buy in three ways:

- Some orders you will write spontaneously in the store, from vendors' catalogs and price lists. These will probably be just replenishment orders.

- Some orders will be written in the store with visiting sales reps. These will also be at least partly for simple replacements (here the rep will often help by taking inventory for you, having a record of your previous orders – the good ones will arrive half-an-hour before the appointment, and have the inventory ready when you are). A visiting rep, moreover, will nearly always have something new to show you, or a special deal to offer, which may not already have come in the mail, or which you may need to be reminded of.

- Some orders will be written by salespeople on your visits to their showrooms. These should not include any inventory replacements, unless you have full and accurate notes of what you need. The buying done in the showroom will be of new lines, or extensions to old lines, and the visit is an opportunity to see the whole range of goods properly displayed. Even for lines you know well, such a visit may give you new ideas on display, or revise your ideas on your selection of pieces (for it is rarely possible to carry a whole line). Showroom visits also provide opportunities to build valuable relationships with principals of vendor companies.

Work within a Budget and, as mentioned under cash flow, schedule deliveries so that you do not get a whole bunch at once, with a consequent peak in cash demand. Also, to repeat the warning given under assortments:

Merchandise in the stockroom does not earn its keep!

Car makers realized years ago the road to profit was "just in time" inventory control, where parts are delivered straight to the production line in the quantities immediately needed, with none in reserve. The same applies to retailing: purchasing must be scheduled so that all merchandise goes straight into the showroom, with none left in the backroom.

Keep up-to-date on which brokers are representing which vendors, because although some vendors will stay with a broker virtually permanently, you may find others represented by different brokers every other year. For this reason, it is best always to think of merchandise in connection with the vendor (who will invoice you), rather than with the broker.

Lastly, always take with you on a buying trip a bunch of Order Numbers, and when the salesperson writes the order on his or her form, get your Order Number on it, and the vendor's name large and clear on your copy. *See* Order Number.

PURCHASING HISTORY. Purchasing History is an integral part of sales analysis. Suffice it to point out here that once, when four out of an inventory of six $300 soup tureens had sold, a poorly programmed computer automatically ordered six more. Unfortunately it had taken four years to sell the four. You will be better informed than that old computer, but the point is clear: Sales Analysis is misleading unless it includes Purchasing History.

R

RATIOS. Ratios show the relationship of expenses to Sales, or of individual Expenses to total Expenses, or of Assets to Liabilities, or any other comparisons which you find useful. They are used both to monitor internal performance, and to compare performance with accepted industry standards.

They are important in themselves, and doubly important when used to compare this year's performance with last.

The most important Ratio is Cost of Goods Sold to Gross Sales, because it determines how much is left (Gross Profit) to meet expenses, but Expenses Ratios are themselves vital in monitoring and controlling performance.

The Income Statement/Profit and Loss Account will itemize expenses, and each expense should be expressed as a percentage of Gross Sales, with comparisons to the previous year. This would have been almost too tedious and expensive to be worthwhile a few years ago, but is now an integral part of most small business software. Computers permit much tighter control and more efficient management than was previously possible, and you need one in order to be competitive.

An important Ratio unrelated to the Income Statement is that for Working Capital, which is the ratio of Current Assets to Current Liabilities, while Return on Invested Capital is the Ratio of Net Income to Long Term Debt plus Owner's Equity (Long Term Debt being liabilities extending beyond one year).

REAL TIME: Almost, but not quite, a synonym for instantaneous. Instantaneous implies that you can get the information you need the instant you want it. It does not necessarily mean that the information is up-to-date. Information available in Real Time is information caught on the fly – what you see is what is happening right now, with all contributing factors built in and fully updated. So to say that computerized bookkeeping can produce real time Net Income Statements is to say that a Statement produced at lunch time will be outdated by one produced at closing time, because merchandise received, sales made, and checks written during the afternoon will all have been taken into account.

RECEIVING, CHECKING IN, and PRICING MERCHANDISE:
All shipments should be processed within twenty-four hours of receipt. To delay just because you know what it is and don't need it till later may cause you to forfeit a damage or shortage claim. Also it may not be what you think, and in any case all merchandise should be on display as quickly as possible: nothing sells from the stock room.

Do not open a delivery unless you have the Purchase Order in hand.

It is essential to mark off receipts on the Purchase Order, so that when items run short you will know if any are still to come and avoid double-ordering (if the vendor sends back-orders), or that you must re-order (if he does not). It is also necessary to ensure that the correct items have been shipped, in the right quantities.

There should be a Packing List, which can be attached to the Purchase Order for the record, or thrown away, unless there is a claim for damage or shortage, when it will be needed.

Damage should be reported to both carrier and vendor, and shortage, of course, to the vendor. If claim instructions are enclosed with the shipment, follow them.

The Invoice may be in or on the carton, in which case it can be passed for payment immediately if everything checks out. Some Invoices will come by mail before the shipment, and some later, but in all cases they must be checked against the marked-off Purchase Order to make sure that you are only being charged for what was actually received, and that the prices match the Purchase Order.

The Invoice is also needed for costing. Your retail prices should remain as stable as possible, with maximum profit margin. As every shipment will have different freight charges, and may have other variations, such as special deals or quantity discounts, it is necessary to cost every Invoice to make sure that it will yield the desired profit at your regular retail price. *See* Costing.

RECONCILING THE BANK STATEMENT: This chore must be done promptly every month. Putting it off can lead to dangerous misinformation on the bank balance, and playing catch-up is extremely tedious. The computer really proves its worth as a time-saver here, but there is one problem which can only be solved by hand, and which considerably lengthens the reconciliation: the credit card companies often lump two or three days' credit card sales together, and they appear as one amount on the bank statement, with much time wasted identifying the daily deposits concerned.

RECONCILING THE REGISTER. This must be done every day without fail. The cash register will total the day's sales, and will show how much has been taken in cash, checks, and credit cards. The cash and checks must be counted and deposited in the bank, and the register's credit card totals must agree with the print-out from the credit card terminal, which will list every transaction, with totals for Master-Card, Visa, American Express, etc.

A convenient way to keep these daily records is to have a Daily Cash Form on which to enter actual against recorded amounts, plus any over/short. The summary tapes from the register and the credit card terminal can be stapled to it, with the individual credit card receipts. This gives a complete summary of the day's transactions, which can be filed in a monthly binder. It may conveniently be combined on one sheet with the Store Diary.

If your bookkeeping is on computer, but not integrated with the Cash Register, the day's transactions from the register print-out can be entered in the General Journal. Total recorded Sales and other income are entered in the Credit Column, balanced in the Debit column by the Bank Deposit, Credit Card Sales and any Petty Cash expenditures.

Your small business software menus may show that you can receive payments and make deposits, but neither is possible unless the sales have been recorded on Invoices generated within the program. As no retail sale is invoiced to the customer (unless you carry charge accounts), this obviously cannot apply.

Advantages of the General Journal method are, first, that the computer will not accept the completed entry if it is not in balance, so errors cannot slip by; secondly, if the cash register shows sales by department, they can be entered separately, producing departmental sales analysis in the monthly Income Statement, and thirdly, it itemizes payment methods (cash, credit cards), and shows cash paid out, so that petty cash payments can be made from the register, and be posted direct to the correct Expense account, without having to keep a separate petty cash account. *See* Petty Cash.

A quick and accurate way to count the cash is to have a fixed sum for the float, say $150. Using a calculator (it is a mistake not to – watch a bank teller) count the coin to an even dollar total, taking out the surplus. Next count the bills, $1's until the total, including coin, is a multiple of 5, $5's to a multiple of 10, then $10's and $20's, up to the $150, taking out the surplus as you go. The total taken out should equal the cash sales on the register tape.

RECORD KEEPING: The primary causes of small business failures are bad record keeping and lack of capital, but the former probably takes priority, because good record keeping protects capital against wastage, and provides the planning data to eke it out if it is slim.

Record keeping must be a daily task. It is the only source of data for financial reports for the business itself, and for tax returns to the School District, City, County, State and the IRS. To neglect it will cause extra work, business errors, worry, and probably tax penalties.

As I point out at every opportunity, the purpose of record keeping is to provide the financial information needed for good management: tax returns, although essential, are the by-products of record keeping, not its purpose.

The first daily tasks are Reconciling the Register and making the bank deposit. These can only be done by the owner or an assistant, but all remaining bookkeeping can, if the owner so wishes, be farmed out to a bookkeeping service or the CPA. This, however, is not desirable, as the owner who does this probably does so because of a dislike or ignorance of bookkeeping, and is therefore unlikely to study or understand the financial reports that come back to him.

With computers and excellent software now available at very reasonable cost, anyone can become a bookkeeper. If needed, basic computer instruction and classes in individual programs are inexpensive, readily available at major computer stores and elsewhere, and will fit even the novice to the task.

Some on-the-job training will still be needed, because even the best software programs will not tell you, for instance, which types of expenditure go to which classes of accounts. This is where a good accountant is essential. He or she, as pointed out under Accountant, must be a person who knows you and your business, so that you can get quick answers on the telephone during the early days, with calls becoming less and less frequent as you become expert.

For those completely new to bookkeeping (and to small business as a whole) the Senior Corps of Retired Executives (S.C.O.R.E.) puts on excellent seminars, and they also provide counseling, a reference library and computer access at their offices. Anyone going into business for the first time will benefit greatly by making use of S.C.O.R.E.'s services and facilities. *See also* Help.

RENOVATION: If you were away from the store for six months, you would probably notice much that needed doing when you returned: stale-looking display, dull paintwork, worn patches in the floor, or whatever. This sort of deterioration can creep up on you unnoticed if you are in the store every day. Make a conscious effort to be alert to the physical condition of the store, and make a point, too, of visiting other stores, particularly new ones, to make sure that you are not unconsciously beginning to let yours become old-fashioned and out-of-date. *See* Paint.

RENT: *see* Lease.

REORDERING: If a customer cannot find what she is looking for she will not ask if it has sold out; she will ask if you have stopped carrying it. If she does not ask she will obviously assume the worst. The lesson is clear: do not run out of things. The frequency and quantity of reorders will, of course, depend on the product, but the principle remains: as long as an item is earning its keep it must be kept in stock without interruption. A reputation for running out of things is the kiss of death, because as well as irritating the customers, it will give the impression that the store is in financial trouble, and that in itself is enough to drive people away.

REPRESENTATIVES: Usually referred to as Reps, or Sales Reps, they can be everything from virtual colleagues to the positively undesirable (such as one who used to lean on the counter ignoring customers, telling dirty jokes, and blowing cigar smoke in my face): a good sales rep will make and keep appointments, keep a record of your previous orders, know what is still outstanding, take inventory of the relevant merchandise before the time of the appointment, and be thoroughly knowledgeable. He or she may also suggest a buying program for the coming year or season, based on the vendor's promotions, your previous sales volume, and upcoming introductions of new lines.

Not all merchandise needs this level of service, and there are many excellent reps providing less. All good reps will find out what you need, suggest new lines that you may want, make sure that you do not over-order (no rep wants a customer resentful at being sold too much), and help with delivery problems.

Some retailers seem to prefer buying without the help of sales reps, as if they fear that the selling power of the rep will overwhelm their own buying judgment. This is a mistake. Sales reps are not merely salespeople: they are invaluable sources of information about their own products, frequently are the source of valuable (or at least interesting) trade gossip, and can be of real help in the retailer's relationship with the vendor.

Friendly relationships with your sales reps are a real asset to your business.

Representatives

RETAIL: It is better to use the word retail rather than price when referring to retail price, as price is sometimes confused with (wholesale) cost.

RETURN ON INVESTMENT, or Return on Invested Capital: Entrepreneurs of the kind who read this book invest a great deal more than money in their businesses. The financial investment is made to achieve other than purely financial goals, so that although the amount of return is important in terms of measuring the health of the business, it may not in itself be the primary concern. Very few small business owners would be able to say, off the cuff, what return the business was getting on its invested capital.

This is a mistake, as it is important in assessing the value and performance of your business, especially in comparison with previous years, and would of course be of extreme importance to a potential purchaser of stock if ever you wished to raise capital, or to a potential purchaser of the business as a whole (and as fate may bring the need for such a person upon you suddenly, it is wise to keep up-to-date in these financial basics).

The formula for Return on Invested Capital is Net Income divided by Owner's Equity plus Long Term Debt (liabilities extending beyond one year).

RETURNS: *see* Complaints.

ROBERT'S RULES OF RETAILING. In the process of writing this book, I gathered a group of essentials, items which have to be close to the heart of any successful retailer. There are many more things which you also have to keep up with, of course, but here are my forget-me-nots:

Premises	*Must be neat, clean, and well maintained.*
Customers	*Must be cultivated for strong growth and long life.*
Staff	*Must be well trained, well treated, and well paid.*
Inventory	*Must be bred and culled like a pedigree herd.*
Credit	*With vendors must be nurtured.*
Bookkeeping	*Must be for management, not merely the IRS.*
The Office	*Must be efficient: documents and data on demand.*
Performance	*Must continually be compared to the previous year.*
Planning	*Must be lifelong, not merely prenatal.*
Personal	*Finance must be separate from business.*

S

SACKS: *see* Bags.

SAFE: For a small retail store, a safe is probably not necessary, unless valuable inventory such as jewelry needs to be locked away at night. A small fire resistant file or cabinet is adequate, particularly now that records are mostly on tape or disk rather than in ledgers. As for cash, a locked cabinet will foil daytime sneak-thieves, and there should never be enough left overnight to justify the cost of a safe.

SALARY: A business owner should treat himself as an employee of his own business and be paid a salary, with appropriate deductions and employer contributions. To help in the start-up and growth phase the salary may be unrealistically small, if it can be supplemented from other sources, but whatever the amount it should be built into the original financial projections and be a normal payroll expense.

The amount of salary will depend on the owner's personal policy. It may be the minimum on which he can survive, with the surplus used for growth, or it may be the maximum upon which the business can survive, allowing for little if any growth, but enabling the owner to invest (or spend) elsewhere. Probably it will be a compromise between the two.

An owner or proprietor can always, of course, draw sums from his own business, but this is bad practice, as it is not structured in any way, and makes budgeting and forecasting impossible. It may also complicate his tax position. (*See also* Employee Leasing.)

SALE: A Sale does not increase Profits. The only point in having a Sale is to get rid of slow-moving inventory, or to give an emergency boost to cash flow. It is better to have cash in the bank than dead inventory on the shelves.

Sidewalk Sales, Anniversary Sales, After-Christmas Sales, New Year's Sales, Remodeling Sales, Pre-Inventory Sales, Introductory Sales, and any other Sales you can think of can all increase cash flow and attract attention and new customers to the store.

Sales should be well advertised, infrequent, and of fixed, preferably short, duration. Frequent sales of vague duration lead to a lack of confidence in the store and loss of reputation.

Preparation for a Sale must be thorough. Sale items must be carefully selected, clearly priced, and attractively displayed. It is a mistake to think that just because items are on sale they can be tossed untidily onto a table (although sometimes a special lucky-dip junk table can be very effective).

If the Sale is for a boost in cash flow rather than to move old inventory it may be desirable to have a Store-Wide Sale. In that case it is best to advertise a single discount for everything, because if there are various discounts for different items, everything will have to be re-priced, which is extremely tedious and time-consuming.

Special Offers and Promotions offered by vendors should not be confused with Sales. They do not reduce profit margins, as you buy them at a discount, and they can be advertised and displayed as something special which you can offer your customers, whereas Sale items will always be perceived as inferior, needing bargain prices to make purchase worthwhile.

SALES ANALYSIS: In the world at large, knowledge is power; in retailing knowledge is profit. It is essential to know what sells and what does not; what sells slowly, and what sells quickly; what sells at Easter, and what sells for Mother's Day.

This knowledge is easily acquired if inventory is classified into departments whose numbers are on the price tag (*see* Pricing Guns), with corresponding numbers on the cash register. Departmental totals will appear on the register's daily print-out, probably with their percentages of total sales.

Given this data, monthly totals can be analyzed at leisure, revealing much profitable information, such as that candy sales were double the average during Easter month, and that 80% of those sales were before Easter itself (actual figures from my own experience).

As to what sells slowly; this belongs in buying analysis rather than Sales Analysis. Sales Analysis will show a department's percentage share of Gross Sales, but if this is suspiciously small, judgment should not be passed without analysis of what has been bought for that department over what period of time. There may have been buying errors, or unforeseen delays in supply.

An unusually large share of Gross Sales may also give a misleading picture of a department's performance, if it is not related to recent buying history. Some special purchase may have inflated a department's sales above normal, but reduced its profit margin.

Some cash registers will give more information than others, from virtually none, to fully integrated inventory control, which will give the sales performance of every item. If the register cannot give the information you need, check your buying records. If you find that there has been consistently strong buying from Widgets International over a fair period of time, analysis of what has been bought will show what to reorder, just as your buying record from another company may show a steady decline in reorders over the same period, indicating that those products have lost their appeal.

SALES PER HOUR: This is a truer measure of performance than monthly sales figures, as it eliminates hidden distortions caused by the varying lengths of the months, holiday closings such as Easter and July 4th, and extra Christmas hours. It is well worth while to make a chart at the beginning of the year, showing the monthly business hours, as these true figures show:

	February	March	% ±
Hours in month	236	263	
Total Sales	17,895.05	17,075.21	–4.58%
Sales per Hour	$75.83	$64.92	–14.38%

The drop of 4.58% in Total Sales might be dismissed as an insignificant bruise, but the X-ray of Sales per Hour reveals much more serious damage: **–14.38%** (!)

The Sales per Hour figure is also a wonderful incentive, because it can provide instantaneous comparison of actual and target figures. (*See* the Sales per Hour Chart, Appendix, p. 186.)

SALES PER SQUARE FOOT. Divide Net Sales by the total rented square footage. The calculation is simple, and ensures that performance can be compared from year to year regardless of any change in the size of the premises. It is important to use the total rented square footage, as sales have to pay for the back-room and office space as well as the showroom, which emphasizes the need to allocate as little space as possible to these two areas.

SALESMANSHIP: Salesmanship is the art of discovering the latent desires of your customers, and matching them to the available merchandise. The style will depend upon the type of store, but the principle remains: find out what the customer wants in a manner which will please her, and match her needs as closely as possible. If there is no easy match, be prepared to offer an alternative. Some customers want to be left alone, and some demand slavish attention, but these are among the latent desires which you must identify before moving on to the merchandise itself.

SALES PEAKS: These will vary depending on the type of business, but every business will have them, and they should be identified and calendared, so that they can be exploited to the full, by adding special inventory, advertising, and perhaps the mounting of Special Events. For a gift shop, the ordinary peaks in the year will be Valentine's Day, Mother's Day, Father's Day, Easter, June Brides, July 4th, Back to School, Halloween, and Christmas. To these can be added the store's anniversary, the State's anniversary, the City's anniversary, and any foreign anniversary which may be appropriate: a store with a French emphasis might celebrate Bastille Day, a British one the Queen's birthday, an Irish one St. Patrick's day, a Scottish one Burns Night, and so on.

SCANNER: If the budget will run to it, a flatbed scanner for incorporating documents or graphics into your computer files will save time, if it saves you typing in text, and will enable you to achieve the otherwise impossible, if you want to use an illustration. Justification for the expense of a scanner will depend upon the extent to which you create such things as brochures, mailers, advertising copy, newsletters or catalogs. *See* Computer, Copy Machine *and* Printer.

SECURITY: There are six security problems:

During business hours:

- Shoplifting
- Hold-up
- Sneak-thief
- Employee theft

After business hours:

- Break-in
- Vandalism

Shoplifting can never be entirely eliminated, but can be minimized by training staff to be alert, by sensible display (do not make impulse thievery easy), by good showroom design (no hidden corners or display units over shoulder height), by mirrors, and, if the cost is justified, by surveillance cameras (or dummies), and by electronic tag detectors at the exit door.

Hold-up cannot be prevented, but staff should be trained to do what the robber says, and to avoid staring at him in case he fears future identification.

Sneak-thieves may target purses or cash in the office or back-room. There should be lockers for purses, and cash should, of course, be well hidden or locked away. It may not be practical to keep the door from the showroom locked, but it should be shut and in full view, not in a hidden corner. If there is a back door, it should be kept locked, and should have either a peep-hole or a small (too small to climb through) window of reinforced glass. It should also have a doorbell, for back-door deliveries.

Employee theft is said to be a major problem in large stores such as supermarkets and department stores. In an owner operated retail store, it should be fully preventable by sound recruiting and good supervision.

Break-in can be discouraged, if not prevented, by good locks, an alarm system, and, if the cost justifies it, by a metal folding grill.

Vandalism is always a risk. The best precaution against it is to choose a location in a good neighborhood, where it is least likely.

The best protection against all risks is a uniformed security guard. If you belong to a merchants' association it may provide such protection for a monthly fee. If not, it is always possible to hire a guard or off-duty policeman for special occasions, or regular peak periods.

It is important to post an Emergency Number on the front door. This should be your, or your manager's, home phone, so that the police can get in touch if necessary. Apart from the fact that owners have been known to go home leaving the front door unlocked, there may be an emergency (a late night dumpster truck driver once rammed a power pole, dragged three air conditioners off the roof and drove off in a panic amid impressive electric fireworks), or they may need permission to act on a suspicion which would not justify them in acting on their own. Don't forget to post a temporary number when you go on vacation.

SELLING YOUR STORE: I have known store owners who, after many successful years and wise personal saving, simply closed the door after a final sale, and went home to happy retirement. Others have handed the business over to sons or daughters, or other favorite members of the family, with whatever financial arrangements best suited them.

Most of us, however, will eventually want to reap the harvest of our labors by selling the business. This raises three questions: *For How Much?*, *To Whom?* and *How Will I Be Paid?*

How Much?

The value of a retail store lies in its assets, physical and financial, in its profitability, in its reputation, and in its name, but a very rough rule of thumb is to value a store at a multiple of annual revenue – five or seven times, depending upon whom you are listening to. Even if you adopt that method, it would be wise to consider the following factors, to see if they back it up.

The value of physical assets, such as inventory, display fixtures, office equipment, etc., and of financial assets (less liabilities) will be shown in the Balance Sheet (*which see*). It is here that good record-keeping over the years will pay off, for if you have the age, original cost, and depreciated value of all your furniture, fixtures and equipment, there need be no haggling over their Balance Sheet figure, and good bookkeeping will ensure the soundness of the financial figures.

Profitability will be shown in Net Income Statements for previous years. Here, more than ever, good bookkeeping shows its worth. The Statements themselves must be readily to hand, backed up by clean records, because a prudent purchaser may well want to see a selection of the original Invoices, etc., on which the Statements are based.

If you have been careful over the years, and avoided federal income tax by plowing profits back into the business, or by rewarding yourself, it is advisable to produce statements showing how, and to what extent, this has been done, so that a potential purchaser can see the disposable profit, and decide how to use it to his own best advantage. This does not suggest in any way that you have been "cooking the books" to avoid tax. It is perfectly legitimate to use profits during the year to expand the business or to increase your own income (not too much: the IRS frowns on excess here), but three or four years of Net Income Statements showing minimal net income, and federal tax returns showing little or no tax, will certainly discourage a potential buyer unless it can be shown that they are the result of a canny use of profit.

There is no formula or even rule of thumb to determine the value of your store's reputation, sometimes called goodwill. It could perhaps be quantified if a mailing list has been developed and used, but this puts a specific value on the mailing list as an asset. The value of reputation must remain a matter for negotiation.

The name of your store, on the other hand, may certainly be valuable. If it is your legal property, registered as a trade mark (the law on this is complex; consult your attorney), then it must specifically be included in the sale if the purchaser of the business wishes to use it. It is perfectly possible to sell a business, but not the name. Again, however, setting a value on the name is a matter for negotiation.

If you have incorporated, the value of the business will be expressed as the value of the stock plus the assets, but stock value still depends upon the factors mentioned above. If you own all the stock, the sale will be quite straightforward, but if you have sold stock to others, their interests must be satisfied. How this is done will depend upon the corporate stockholders' agreement, and it is essential that this be drawn up and agreed by all stockholders as early in the life of the corporation as possible. Without such an agreement, minority stockholders can refuse any offer put to them by you or the purchaser, and are free to keep their stock, or dispose of it to anyone else by gift or sale, making it impossible for you, the majority stockholder, to offer a clean and complete deal to a purchaser.

To Whom?

You will almost certainly receive unsolicited mail from brokers offering to value and sell your business for you, just as you may receive offers from realtors to sell your house, or you may go looking for a broker yourself. By all means check out the details: no harm is done, and a good sale may result. However, a fee will be charged by most business brokers, whether or not a sale is consummated, so explore this route with care.

Obvious possible buyers are existing stockholders, family, friends, and employees, but financing may be a problem here.

A classified ad in the appropriate newspaper or trade magazine may bring promising inquiries, and if you are a member of a merchants' association, or any other trade association or club, some discreet networking may produce results.

The search will depend very much on the type of business: florists, gift shops and hardware stores probably attract quite different sorts of people, but beware of investors from unrelated fields who coldly analyze financial statements and detect possibilities of profit, but who have no personal interest in, or knowledge of, retailing.

How Will I Be Paid?

It is common for the seller of a business to agree to payments out of future income, but this is risky. The economy is unpredictable, and even if it remains good, a fire, or sickness, or the unexpected incompetence of the buyer, may reduce the income, or even eliminate it.

A promissory note gives you a right to legal action, but cannot produce money which, whether by bad luck or villainy, simply is not there.

Unless you have good reason to have cast-iron confidence (and not mere faith) in the honesty, ability, and financial soundness of the purchaser, it is best to require payment in full upon the closing of the sale.

Unfortunately, whichever payment method you select will have tax advantages or disadvantages. You final decision will depend upon your personal circumstances and the advice of your CPA.

SEMI MONTHLY: *see* Bimonthly.

SHIPPING: Readiness to ship your customers' purchases creates much good will, and if you are shipping out of state, may well save them Sales Tax as well. If you save some cartons and the packing material from incoming shipments, it may not be necessary to buy any. Even for small quantities per week, it is worth arranging for automatic pick-up by UPS or whatever service is most convenient. Keep scales and a rate card by the cash register, for quick service, add 2 lb. to the actual weight, to allow for carton and packaging weight, and put on a small percentage for "handling" – the labor cost of packing etc. If the customer orders in the store, ask her to write the shipping label, to eliminate any comeback from misaddressing or bad handwriting. Make sure that any gift tags are attached, and do the actual packing in the back room, where all necessary materials are to hand.

If the shipment is from a mail or telephone order, and to be sent to the customer herself, the receipt can be enclosed, but if it is to be sent as a gift, mail the receipt and confirmation of recipient's name and address to the purchaser.

Enclose at least a "Thank You" or "With Compliments" card with every shipment, and if there is a store brochure it should most certainly be included.

Do not put elaborate bows on giftwraps to be shipped. They only get crushed and make a depressing impression when unpacked.

SHORTAGE: Some shipments may not contain all that is on the Packing List or the Invoice. *See* Receiving, Checking In *and* Pricing Merchandise.

SHORT-SHIPPED: same as Shortage.

SIDEWALK SALE: *see* Sale.

SIGNS: The name of the store must be on the front of the building, either on the structure or on an awning, and if you are in a strip center there may also be a big free-standing sign listing all the stores. Dimensions and background color for both the store-front and the free-standing sign will probably be specified in the lease, but type-style and logo will, of course, be your own.

The store-front name on the building can be self-lit, if the lease and the budget allow it. On an awning, "show-through" lettering, illuminated from behind, is very effective.

If there is an awning, it is necessary to have a sign beneath it at right angles to the store front, so that walking shoppers can more easily find you.

Free-standing signs are frequently subject to city licensing fees. If the landlord owns the sign, the charge may be included in the CAM (Common Area Maintenance) charge, or shown separately.

SOFTWARE: *see* Computers.

SOLE PROPRIETOR: *see* Proprietor.

SOLICITORS. A small notice on the door is the best way to discourage those who come in with offers such as fabulous warehouse close-out prices on the merchandise they have in the trunk of their cars. They are merely a nuisance if you are alone in the store, but can be a problem if they start trying to sell their wares to staff or customers.

SOME ASSEMBLY REQUIRED: Many display units, and much furniture and shelving, will arrive packed flat, and need to be assembled. Be prepared. There will nearly always be an instruction sheet and a bag of nuts, bolts and odd little fittings, and special tools, such as Allen keys (those little hexagon-section L-shaped rods) will probably be included, but the usual bland assurance that you will need no more than a hammer and a screwdriver is optimistic. To avoid delay and confusion, the store should have, of course, a hammer, but there should also be large, medium and small screwdrivers, both flat and Phillips, plus a pair of pliers, a crescent wrench, and, for general layout purposes, a 25 ft. (minimum) steel tape. The handyman owner will also find that most of his tools from home will gradually gravitate to the store unless he is careful. He should make the store buy its own tools as needed.

Those who are not comfortable using tools must plan ahead, so as to have someone on call to assemble a new unit when it arrives. The purpose of any new unit is to increase sales, efficiency and profit; delay in putting it to use wastes money.

SPECIAL ORDERS. An excellent way to build business is to offer a Special Order service for items or quantities which would not normally be carried (not to be confused with Call Cards, which are for standard items temporarily out of stock). It is seldom possible to carry an entire product range, but with the vendor's catalog and price-list handy, it is easy to identify a customer's special need and include it with the next stock order, or, if the quantity is large enough, a Purchase Order can be raised immediately. The independent small retailer can offer much quicker and more flexible service in this way than even the best department stores, where the size of the organization inevitably leads to slowness and rigidity.

A three or four part serially numbered Sales Order form is needed – one for the customer, one to be filed alphabetically by customer, one alphabetically by vendor, and perhaps one for a master numerical file, in case the others go astray. The order must be accurately entered and priced, with Sales Tax, the customer must be asked for a deposit, preferably 50%, and estimated delivery time *must* be stated. When the order is placed with the vendor, the P.O. Number will be entered on the Sales Order copies, and the Sales Order number on the P.O.

Do not ask the customer to fill in her own name and address on the Order Form; it may be illegible, and she may put it in the wrong place. Make sure that the telephone number will get her during the day, so that you can call her during your business hours.

When the goods come in, call the customer, and put the goods with a copy of the Sales Order in a specified place, so that anyone who works in the store knows where to find them.

STATEMENT: Each shipment of merchandise will be billed on an Invoice, and at the end of every month most vendors will send a Statement of Account, listing all unpaid Invoices, any payments you have made, and any Credits owing (although some vendors' invoices will say "Please pay from this Invoice. No Statement will be sent"). Most Statements will also indicate how much of the balance due is Current, and how much overdue by 30, 60, and 90 days. *The Statement is not a bill.* It is only what it says it is, a Statement. Payment should be made only against the actual Invoices which your own records show as outstanding. These should normally match the Statement, but payment for an Invoice may have crossed the Statement in the mail, and show as still outstanding, or a credit for damaged goods may not be shown: to accept the Statement total would then, of course, result in overpayment. The document of accounting record is always the Invoice, not the Statement, which should simply be reconciled with your own records. In a well kept computer file, this can be done at the touch of a button.

It is a courtesy to the vendor (and courtesy to vendors is seldom wasted) to use return portions of Statements, if any.

STATIONERY. Many first-time store owners spend much time, and worse, money, on the design of an impressive letterhead. This is a waste. You will write few letters to customers, and it is prompt payment, not fancy stationery, that will impress vendors. Your computer will provide all that is needed.

You will probably find it quicker and easier to write Purchase Orders by hand, rather than on the computer, so you will need Purchase Order forms. These and other standard items such as shipping labels and Sales Order forms (for customers' special orders) can be purchased quite inexpensively from any mail order office supply house, printed with your store name and address. They should be numbered, with some more unnumbered for continuation sheets.

The only custom stationery you need is a business card, for which design is important. This does not mean that it has to be elaborate or expensive, but it must be good. For customers, a card seems almost as effective a reminder as a more informative brochure, and a supply beside the cash register dwindles quickly. We all have a stack (if not an organized file!) of business cards, but where do we keep that fancy brochure we picked up in a store last week?

For vendors, and other business contacts, a well designed business card will be a reminder of your manner and appearance, and perpetuate the impression which you wanted to convey.

STATISTICS. Some statistics, over and above those required for the Financial Statement and the IRS, are needed for good management. No statistic, however, is of any value unless it is used. Detailed Sales Analysis, for instance, is wasted unless it is used in decisions on inventory levels and purchasing.

Management, however, is as much art as science. Some managers base every decision on statistical analysis, others fly by the seat of their pants. Most fall somewhere in between, but the ones who succeed are those who feel a need for information in decision-making, and take the trouble to get it. Those who don't bother, fail.

See Decision Making, Ratios, Sales Analysis, Sales per Hour, Sales per Square Foot, etc.

T

TAXES. If you fall behind on obligations to vendors, there is usually room for negotiation. If you fall behind in paying taxes, there may be limited room for negotiation, but penalties mount, and eventual retribution is severe and certain. Carelessness in meeting tax deadlines can cost a prosperous business dearly, and inability to meet tax deadlines is a sign of serious trouble.

The best way to avoid tax problems is to keep accurate, up-to-date, financial records, preferably on a computer, so that Taxable and Nontaxable sales, for instance, are totaled automatically from the daily entries, and the figures can be brought up with just a few key-strokes at the end of the month.

If there is some difficulty in meeting a deadline, ask for help. Nothing will reduce or cancel your obligation, but arrangements can sometimes be made. The worst course is to do nothing. Hell hath no fury like a tax man ignored (unless it be a Credit Manager.)

TELEPHONE. Money can be saved by shopping around, but do not stint on a phone system. Get the equipment you need. Most small stores probably need a phone at the register, in the office, and in the stock room, with intercom capability and an extra line so that customers calling in do not get a busy signal. A cordless phone is extremely useful, as it allows you to walk round the showroom while finding the answers to callers' questions.

Separate lines will be needed for the fax machine and the credit card terminal.

If the budget does not run to a full system to begin with, make sure that what you do install can be expanded later. Good communications within a business are as important as oil in an engine.

TEMPORARY STAFF. Christmas, office backlogs, and taking inventory are the most likely events to need temporary help.

Summer is not usually a busy time for retail stores, so it is difficult to give work to deserving students looking for summer jobs. They may, however, be glad of an offer of Christmas work, so give out job applications and keep them on file.

Specialized temporary help for the office, such as for bookkeeping or data entry, is best found through a professional agency, but for other events such as taking inventory it may be possible to call on one's own, or staff's, friends.

Temporary staff should not usually be paid as casual or contract labor, without any deductions. This could lead to tax problems. Consult your CPA as to the correct payment classification and payment method in each case. *See also* Employee Leasing.

TERMS. Somewhere on the Invoice, usually in one of a line of little boxes showing Order Date, Order Number, etc., will be the word Terms, short for Terms of Business, which may be anything from c.o.d. to Net 90 days. Abide by the Terms, and take advantage of discounts. 1/10 Net 30, for instance, allows you to deduct 1% if the Invoice is paid in 10 days. On one Invoice this does not amount to much; taken at every opportunity over the year it will make a worthwhile improvement in Gross Profit.

You cannot unilaterally take a discount if you pay early (*see* No Anticipation), nor should you pay early at all. If terms are 30 days, pay in 30 days, and have the use of the money in the meantime. Part of your Working Capital is generated by the gap between customers paying you cash on the barrel-head, and you not paying your vendors for 30 days. Do not needlessly reduce this advantage.

TIME CLOCK. *See* Clocking On.

TIME MANAGEMENT. As owner and operator of a business, you are working for that most difficult of all employers, yourself. You report only to that face you see in the mirror every morning, and one of the surest ways of ensuring that it will be a cheerful encounter is to manage your time efficiently. Organizing a closet always seems to make more room, and it is the same with time.

The real benefit of Time Management, however, is that it ensures that the essential administrative routine is taken care of, so that you can concentrate comfortably on more creative activities for the rest of the day, such as planning, purchasing, and, above all, spending time with the customers. These are the prime duties of the retail store owner, but, like motherhood, they cannot be properly attended to until the chores are done.

An object lesson in the perils of not defining and organizing the job was provided by the prospective buyer of a retail store with a small staff, who was asked how he would run it. It was apparent that the question surprised him, for he had to think for a few moments, and then said "Well, I suppose I shall just have to coordinate and supervise." He was out of business in less than two years. On the other hand, an old friend who had a hardware store used to get up at 4:30 a.m. every day, and have all his office work done before opening at nine, so that he could spend the day with his customers.

Time Management

TOOLS and EQUIPMENT: *see* Some Assembly Required.

TRAINING: Friends, relatives, and part-time workers such as house-wives, so often the backbone of a small retail enterprise, are seldom trainable. They are usually mature confident people who firmly believe that reasonable intelligence and common sense are all that is needed in a non-technical business such as retailing – particularly a small one. This can cause problems. First, because two or three equally intelligent people may come up with different methods for the same process, which will obviously lead to confusion and inconsistency, and secondly, because their methods may anyway not be the best.

There are no solutions to this problem except tact (which includes listening, in case someone does indeed have a better way) and persever-ance. If you do identify a problem, it can only be solved by convincing and tactful demonstration that the way you want the job done is going either to benefit the business or make the job easier – and if it does one it will probably do the other. The fatal mistake is to insist that everything be done your way simply because that's the way you want it, without explaining why.

However hard you try, though, some people will never be taught some tasks. Reloading a pricing gun may be out of reach of a brilliant salesperson, or gift wrapping quite beyond the abilities of another. Build on peoples' strengths, adapt to their weaknesses, and be ready to learn from them yourself.

TRADE ASSOCIATIONS. Join those which will help your business. Do not waste subscriptions on any whose benefits to you cannot be identified. Benefits may not be financial: membership can be of real help in bringing you into a network of fellow merchants, and attendance at meetings will keep you abreast of local developments. You do not want to be taken by surprise when the next block is demolished for construction of a new shopping center, and friendship with neighbors should always be cultivated. State and national associations which claim to protect and advance the interests of small business in the legislature should be judged on the merits of their agendas. You must judge whether your subscription will advance your own interests. *See* Chamber of Commerce.

TRIPLE NET. A Lease at Triple Net includes three charges over and above the basic rent: Common Area Maintenance, Insurance, and Property Taxes. *See* Lease.

U – Z

UMBRELLAS. A customer who has been helped to her car in a blinding rain storm will come back in all weathers. Keep an umbrella handy to provide the personal service which enables the independent retailer to prosper against department and discount store competition.

A convenient place for customers to park their own dripping umbrellas will also make life just that little bit smoother for both them and you. Other things being equal, the store with most comfort and convenience will come out ahead.

UPS. United Parcel Service or Uninterruptible Power Supply. Both are important. United Parcel Service will deliver much of your merchandise, and if you do any amount at all of shipping for customers it is worth while to sign up with UPS for automatic daily pick-up. There is a small weekly fee over and above the actual shipping charge, but it is cheaper and much more convenient than asking for pick-ups individually, and well worth it in time saved from taking parcels to the post office.

Uninterruptible Power Supply for the computer may not be essential provided you back up your data to tape or disk regularly. This sort of UPS is battery powered and fairly expensive, but it does ensure that no data is lost if the power fails while you are working. The average small retailer, however, will probably not have a sufficiently large back log of work during a day to make a UPS necessary. The real need for UPS arises if the computer is programmed to work unattended during the night.

VACATIONS. Fix vacation dates as early in the year as possible, particularly your own. Employees will normally acknowledge the boss's right to first choice of vacation dates, but it is only fair to make them known as soon as possible. It is also necessary to plan the year ahead so that everyone can be informed of no-vacation periods, to cover any Special Events which will require all hands on deck.

VENDOR: The company which supplies the goods, and which you pay: not necessarily the same as the one that took the order. Purchase

Orders must always bear the Vendor's name, and be filed accordingly, so that they can be pulled and checked when the goods arrive.

WE/YOU. An employee once said to me, when she saw the cash register total, "You did very well today." This made me aware that I was doing something wrong. With good incentives, properly administered, and thoughtful management, she would have said "We did very well today." The difference between We and You is the difference between a warm, welcoming and lively store, and a dull one. It is also the difference between maximum and minimum profit.

Vendor

WHOLESALE. You sell to your customers at Retail, and buy from your Vendors at Wholesale. "Wholesale," however, is not a precise term. It may be Net, or Net less Promotional Discount, or at List less Discount; it may be Freight Paid, or less 2% if paid in 10 days, then

Net 30, and there are many other variations. If you are not buying direct from the factory the Wholesale Price may also vary from vendor to vendor, and a vendor may have different prices for the same item, depending on quantity, or on the status of your store. If you handle foodstuffs, for instance, you may get advantageous supermarket prices if you order in sufficiently large quantities. Never take "Wholesale" at face value.

WINDOWS. Keep them clean, not forgetting the inside: dried condensation and dead flies can create a very seedy appearance. This means that the inside will have to be easily accessible. *See* Display.

WORKING CAPITAL *see* Capital.

WORLD WIDE WEB: Knowledge is power, and Webmanship, if I may coin a word, opens up such a world of knowledge that it has become virtually an essential skill for the retail store owner. For instance

http://www.retailadvz.com/frrtop.htm

will bring up a web page called The Retail Business Resource Center, which is well worth a visit. It has a dated newsletter, and a schedule of workshops such as "My Customers Are Not Buying!!" and "Specialty Store Buyer's Workshop," plus what they call Live Business Chat sessions, which are interactive.

A thorough net surfing session may well turn up other useful sites, and of course the web is a wonderful tool for digging out information which you cannot find any other way – or at least not without a great deal of time, trouble and visits to libraries. Cultivate your *Webmanship!*

XEROX: *see* Copy Machine.

XMAS: *see* Christmas.

YIELD. The amount which will be realized at retail if every item on an invoice is sold. The Total of an Invoice, expressed as a percentage of the Yield, will give you Gross Profit. *e.g. If goods are bought at list (suggested retail) less discount:*

Goods, at list	$2,000 (as List is Retail, this is **Yield**)
Less 50%	$1,000
Net goods total	$1,000
Freight	30
Total Payable	1,030 = 51.5% of Yield

Gross Profit = 48.5%

Or if goods are bought at net:

Net Goods	$1,000
Freight	30
Total payable (TDC)	$1,030
Yield at Keystone (2 × TDC)	$2,060

Gross Profit = 50%

As in this case you have bought at net you are free "to Keystone it," *i.e.* double the True Delivered Cost, and achieve the full 50% Gross Profit, including freight.

For goods bought at List, calculation of Yield monitors the erosion of Gross Profit by freight, and for goods bought at net it is the only way to arrive at accurate retail prices, and maintain overall Gross Profit. Accurate prices are those which reflect the appropriate profit margin for the particular item. They may be adjusted upwards (if the value is there), or downwards if an exceptional rate of sale justifies a smaller margin, but no retail price can be fixed without the accurate base price to work from.

ZIP CODE enables you to analyze your customer base. Even if you do no mailing, knowledge of where your customers come from will help in deciding where to aim your advertising (your photocopied checks will provide the addresses you need for this purpose), and may even guide you to a new, or branch, location.

Appendix

Sample charts which you will find useful:

Sales per Hour — *Your Monthly Performance Monitor*

For opening 9–6 Mon–Sat, 12–5 Sunday,
plus 9am–8pm Mon–Fri from 1st Monday in December through the 23rd.

1998	Business Hours	TOTAL SALES	Sales per Hour	Taxable Sales % of Total	Non-taxable Sales % of Total	Month's Sales as % of Year‡
JAN	254					
FEB	245					
MAR	259					
APR	249					
MAY	263					
JUN	250					
JUL	254					
AUG	263					
SEP	250					
OCT	263					
NOV	245					
DEC	273					
YEAR	3068					

‡To be calculated only at end of year.

Jan	Closed	New Year's Day
Apr	"	Easter Sunday
July	"	July 4th (Thursday)
Nov	"	Thanksgiving
Dec	"	Christmas Day and the following day (Wed. & Thurs.) + 32 hrs. (16 late evenings)

Deadlines/Reminders

Federal, State, County, City & School District authorities all want some of your money, and impose penalties if they do not get it on time. Some of the most important and usual forms are listed below. The full Federal list is available from the IRS, *Publication 509*, but State and Local requirements will, of course, vary. Your CPA can be of the greatest help in the accurate and timely filing of all returns.

A suggested chart of deadlines is given overleaf. It is helpful to see them all at once as well as in your calendar, where they are scattered, and you can also show reminders of Rent, Insurance, etc. All payroll returns, of course, cease to concern you if you are a client of an Employee Leasing company (*which see*).

FEDERAL:

Form 941 (FICA). Social Security, Medicare, Withholding. Pay deposits monthly (by 15th) to your bank (which is acting as a Federal Depository), with a coupon* and submit the Report quarterly.

Form 940 (FUTA): Unemployment Tax. Payable on the first $7,000 of each employee's earnings. Pay by coupon for every $100 total liability incurred, and submit Report annually.

Form W-2. For each employee. Annual.

Form 1099. Annual: most commonly for Contract Labor, but other 1099's are for Interest, Dividends, Abandoned Property, etc. Consult your CPA.

Form I-9 & W-4. For new employees. Essential records for INS or IRS on demand, not sent.

Form 1120 for annual <u>Corporate</u> Income Tax return: estimated tax must be paid Quarterly by coupon. Other business structures will of course need different forms. Again, consult your CPA.

STATE:

Sales Tax: Payable annually, quarterly, or monthly, depending on sales volume.

Franchise Tax: Annual. In effect, if not in name, State corporate Income Tax.

Form C3. Texas Employment Commission. State Unemployment Tax. (The form number and commission name are about to be changed).

CITY and SCHOOL DISTRICT

These will demand Property Tax annually, payable by January 31st for the previous year:

---

*Out of the coupon book, about the size of a check-book, which you will receive from the IRS with all your other forms. The coupon is designed for deposits on various taxes: you fill in the appropriate "bubble" to indicate what tax you are paying, and for which payment period, but use a separate coupon for each tax.

Deadlines/Reminders Chart

Shown with sample entries. Actual entries will depend on the nature and structure of your business, and on state regulations. *"Coupon"* indicates that intermediate deposits are made with a coupon before the final Return is due. See previous page for coupon description

PAYMENT DUE, or TASK	Bimonthly	Monthly	Quarterly	Annually	Date
Rent		✗			1st of month
Reconcile Bank Statement		✗			A.S.A.P.
Sales Tax			✗		20th after end of Qtr.
Form 1120. Fed. Corp. Inc. Tax. Return for prev. year.					March 15th (not April)
Form 1120. Est. Tax for current year. Coupon.					4/15, 6/15, 9/15, 12/15
Form 940. Fed Unemployment (FUTA). Coupon.			✗		By end of month after Qtr. if more than $100 due
Form 940. Fed. Unemployment (FUTA). Return.				✗	January 31st
Form 941. SS, Medicare, Withholding (FICA). Coupon.		✗			15th, for previous month
Form 941. Return.			✗		By end of month after Qtr.
Form 1099, payments to non-employees, to them.				✗	January 31st
Form 1099. Copies to IRS.				✗	February 28th
Form 1096. Summary of 1099's to IRS.				✗	February 28th
Form I9. Not sent, but must be on file.					When hired
Form W2, to employees.				✗	January 31st
Form W3. Wage & Tax Statements + W2 copies.				✗	February 28th
Form W4. Not sent, but must be on file.					When hired

State Franchise Tax				X	May 15th
State Form C3. State Unemployment			X		By end of month after Qtr.
Payroll (for bimonthlies)	X				15th & 31st
Insurance		X			
Electricity		X			
Gas		X			
Water		X			
Telephone		X			

Plus any other regular payments you may wish to add, such as credit cards.

Monday	Tuesday	Wednesday	Thursday	Friday	Saturday	Sunday

Call Cards

VENDOR .... DATE ....

CUSTOMER ....

TEL: HOME .... WORK ....

Use back for address & other information

<u>**WANTS:**</u>

In a perfect world you would never be out of stock of anything, but in real life you will disappoint customers because you are waiting for a shipment. This can be turned almost to advantage by using Call Cards, showing the customer's name, address, telephone number and needs.

The cards are filed by vendor, to be pulled when the next order is placed (or with it if already outstanding), so the vendor's name, not the customer's, must be at the top. The Purchase Order should be cross-referenced to the Call Card, and the customer is called when the goods come in.

The advantage of this system is not only that it gets the customer what she wants, but also that it impresses her enormously when she is called, and you get a reputation for exceptional service.

The customer should not fill out the Call Card herself, as her writing may be illegible, and in any case the cards need to be in standard form, and she will probably put information in the wrong places.

Call Cards are for merchandise which will be on order for regular inventory. They should not be confused with Special Orders.

One-Step Retail Pricing from Net Cost of Items Invoiced Singly

To find Retail on a single item, in the range of freight charges and profit margins shown below, select the Freight Percentage in the left hand column, and the desired Profit Margin in the top row, and multiply the net cost of the item by the figure shown.

Margin:	50%	47.5%	45%	42.5%	40%	37.5%	35%	32.5%	30%	27.5%	25%
Freight: 0.0%	2.00	1.90	1.82	1.74	1.67	1.60	1.54	1.48	1.43	1.38	1.33
2.5%	2.05	1.95	1.86	1.78	1.71	1.64	1.58	1.52	1.46	1.41	1.37
→ 5.0%	2.10	2.00	1.91	1.83	*1.75*	1.68	1.62	1.56	1.50	1.45	1.40
7.5%	2.15	2.05	1.95	1.87	1.79	1.72	1.65	1.59	1.54	1.48	1.43
10.0%	2.20	2.10	2.00	1.91	1.83	1.76	1.69	1.63	1.57	1.52	1.47
12.5%	2.25	2.14	2.05	1.96	1.88	1.80	1.73	1.67	1.61	1.55	1.50
15.0%	2.30	2.19	2.09	2.00	1.92	1.84	1.77	1.70	1.64	1.59	1.53

Example: if the net cost is $7.50 and the freight is 5%, the Retail Price at 40% Profit Margin will be $7.50 × 1.75 = $13.12, which you could round up to $13.25, or down to $12.99 depending on the character of the item.

Explanation:

Retail price		$13.12
Item cost	$7.50	
Freight @ 5%	.37	
TDC	$7.87	(7.87)
Profit (40% of $13.12)		$5.25

One-Step Retail Pricing per Piece, from Case Cost, Including Freight

The following seven tables enable you to multiply case cost, whatever it may be, by a single figure, to get retail per piece at the desired profit margin, including freight (at 0%, 2.5%, 5%, 7.5%, 10%, 12.5% and 15% of net invoice cost), and in case contents from 6 to 144 pieces.

Method: Select the table for the appropriate freight percentage (this one is for 0%). Select case quantity in Column 1, and desired Margin in the top row. To get retail per piece, at full desired margin on delivered cost, multiply net case cost by the percentage shown.

Example on facing page: Freight = 0%

Case contents = 12

Desired margin = 40%

Case cost, say $60,

Retail per piece @ 40% margin is $60 × .1389 = **$8.33**

Explanation: The formula is based on a retail yield of $100 for the whole case. Divide that by case quantity to get retail per piece (e.g. $100 ÷ 12 = $8.33), and express that $8.33 as a fraction of case cost, which must be $60, if retail yield is $100 @ 40% margin; .1389 × 60 is $8.33, which gives 40% margin on the $5 per piece net cost (60 ÷ 12).

0%
Freight

One-Step Retail Pricing per Piece, Including Freight
for Merchandise Purchased by the Case

Markup:	50%	47.5%	45%	42.5%	40% ↓	37.5%	35%	32.5%	30%	27.5%	25%	22.5%	20%
Case Quan: 6	.3333	.3175	.3030	.2899	.2778	.2667	.2564	.2469	.2381	.2299	.2222	.2151	.2083
10	.2000	.1905	.1818	.1739	.1667	.1600	.1538	.1481	.1429	.1379	.1333	.1290	.1250
→ 12	.1667	.1587	.1515	.1449	*.1389*	.1333	.1282	.1235	.1190	.1149	.1111	.1075	.1042
16	.1250	.1190	.1136	.1087	.1042	.1000	.0962	.0926	.0893	.0862	.0833	.0806	.0781
18	.1111	.1058	.1010	.0966	.0926	.0889	.0855	.0823	.0794	.0766	.0741	.0717	.0694
20	.1000	.0952	.0909	.0870	.0833	.0800	.0769	.0741	.0714	.0690	.0667	.0645	.0625
24	.0833	.0794	.0758	.0725	.0694	.0667	.0641	.0617	.0595	.0575	.0556	.0538	.0521
30	.0667	.0635	.0606	.0580	.0556	.0533	.0513	.0494	.0476	.0460	.0444	.0430	.0417
32	.0625	.0595	.0568	.0543	.0521	.0500	.0481	.0463	.0446	.0431	.0417	.0403	.0391
35	.0571	.0544	.0519	.0497	.0476	.0457	.0440	.0423	.0408	.0394	.0381	.0369	.0357
36	.0556	.0529	.0505	.0483	.0463	.0444	.0427	.0412	.0397	.0383	.0370	.0358	.0347
40	.0500	.0476	.0455	.0435	.0417	.0400	.0385	.0370	.0357	.0345	.0333	.0323	.0313
48	.0417	.0397	.0379	.0362	.0347	.0333	.0321	.0309	.0298	.0287	.0278	.0269	.0260
60	.0333	.0317	.0303	.0290	.0278	.0267	.0256	.0247	.0238	.0230	.0222	.0215	.0208
72	.0278	.0265	.0253	.0242	.0231	.0222	.0214	.0206	.0198	.0192	.0185	.0179	.0174
96	.0208	.0198	.0189	.0181	.0174	.0167	.0160	.0154	.0149	.0144	.0139	.0134	.0130
144	.0139	.0132	.0126	.0121	.0116	.0111	.0107	.0103	.0099	.0096	.0093	.0090	.0087

Example shown: *For case of 12 at 40% margin, multiply net case cost by .1389 to get retail per piece.*

**2.5%
Freight**

One-Step Retail Pricing per Piece, Including Freight
for Merchandise Purchased by the Case

Markup:	50%	47.5%	45%	42.5%	40%	37.5%	35%	32.5%	30%	27.5%	25%	22.5%	20%
Case Quan: 6	.3417	.3254	.3106	.2971	.2847	.2733	.2628	.2531	.2440	.2356	.2278	.2204	.2135
10	.2050	.1952	.1864	.1783	.1708	.1640	.1577	.1519	.1464	.1414	.1367	.1323	.1281
12	.1708	.1627	.1553	.1486	*.1424*	.1367	.1314	.1265	.1220	.1178	.1139	.1102	.1068
16	.1281	.1220	.1165	.1114	.1068	.1025	.0986	.0949	.0915	.0884	.0854	.0827	.0801
18	.1139	.1085	.1035	.0990	.0949	.0911	.0876	.0844	.0813	.0785	.0759	.0735	.0712
20	.1025	.0976	.0932	.0891	.0854	.0820	.0788	.0759	.0732	.0707	.0683	.0661	.0641
24	.0854	.0813	.0777	.0743	.0712	.0683	.0657	.0633	.0610	.0589	.0569	.0551	.0534
30	.0683	.0651	.0621	.0594	.0569	.0547	.0526	.0506	.0488	.0471	.0456	.0441	.0427
32	.0641	.0610	.0582	.0557	.0534	.0513	.0493	.0475	.0458	.0442	.0427	.0413	.0400
35	.0586	.0558	.0532	.0509	.0488	.0469	.0451	.0434	.0418	.0404	.0390	.0378	.0366
36	.0569	.0542	.0518	.0495	.0475	.0456	.0438	.0422	.0407	.0393	.0380	.0367	.0356
40	.0513	.0488	.0466	.0446	.0427	.0410	.0394	.0380	.0366	.0353	.0342	.0331	.0320
48	.0427	.0407	.0388	.0371	.0356	.0342	.0329	.0316	.0305	.0295	.0285	.0276	.0267
60	.0342	.0325	.0311	.0297	.0285	.0273	.0263	.0253	.0244	.0236	.0228	.0220	.0214
72	.0285	.0271	.0259	.0248	.0237	.0228	.0219	.0211	.0203	.0196	.0190	.0184	.0178
96	.0214	.0203	.0194	.0186	.0178	.0171	.0164	.0158	.0153	.0147	.0142	.0138	.0133
144	.0142	.0136	.0129	.0124	.0119	.0114	.0110	.0105	.0102	.0098	.0095	.0092	.0089

Example shown: *For case of 12 at 40% margin, multiply net case cost by .1424 to get retail per piece.*

5% Freight

One-Step Retail Pricing per Piece, Including Freight
for Merchandise Purchased by the Case

Markup:	50%	47.5%	45%	42.5%	40%	37.5%	35%	32.5%	30%	27.5%	25%	22.5%	20%
Case Quan: 6	.3500	.3333	.3182	.3043	.2917	.2800	.2692	.2593	.2500	.2414	.2333	.2258	.2188
10	.2100	.2000	.1909	.1826	.1750	.1680	.1615	.1556	.1500	.1448	.1400	.1355	.1313
12	.1750	.1667	.1591	.1522	*.1458*	.1400	.1346	.1296	.1250	.1207	.1167	.1129	.1094
16	.1313	.1250	.1193	.1141	.1094	.1050	.1010	.0972	.0938	.0905	.0875	.0847	.0820
18	.1167	.1111	.1061	.1014	.0972	.0933	.0897	.0864	.0833	.0805	.0778	.0753	.0729
20	.1050	.1000	.0955	.0913	.0875	.0840	.0808	.0778	.0750	.0724	.0700	.0677	.0656
24	.0875	.0833	.0795	.0761	.0729	.0700	.0673	.0648	.0625	.0603	.0583	.0565	.0547
30	.0700	.0667	.0636	.0609	.0583	.0560	.0538	.0519	.0500	.0483	.0467	.0452	.0438
32	.0656	.0625	.0597	.0571	.0547	.0525	.0505	.0486	.0469	.0453	.0438	.0423	.0410
35	.0600	.0571	.0545	.0522	.0500	.0480	.0462	.0444	.0429	.0414	.0400	.0387	.0375
36	.0583	.0556	.0530	.0507	.0486	.0467	.0449	.0432	.0417	.0402	.0389	.0376	.0365
40	.0525	.0500	.0477	.0457	.0438	.0420	.0404	.0389	.0375	.0362	.0350	.0339	.0328
48	.0438	.0417	.0398	.0380	.0365	.0350	.0337	.0324	.0313	.0302	.0292	.0282	.0273
60	.0350	.0333	.0318	.0304	.0292	.0280	.0269	.0259	.0250	.0241	.0233	.0226	.0219
72	.0292	.0278	.0265	.0254	.0243	.0233	.0224	.0216	.0208	.0201	.0194	.0188	.0182
96	.0219	.0208	.0199	.0190	.0182	.0175	.0168	.0162	.0156	.0151	.0146	.0141	.0137
144	.0146	.0139	.0133	.0127	.0122	.0117	.0112	.0108	.0104	.0101	.0097	.0094	.0091

Example shown: *For case of 12 at 40% margin, multiply net case cost by .1458 to get retail per piece.*

**7.5%
Freight**

One-Step Retail Pricing per Piece, Including Freight for Merchandise Purchased by the Case

Markup:	50%	47.5%	45%	42.5%	40%	37.5%	35%	32.5%	30%	27.5%	25%	22.5%	20%
Case Quan: 6	.3583	.3413	.3258	.3116	.2986	.2867	.2756	.2654	.2560	.2471	.2389	.2312	.2240
10	.2150	.2048	.1955	.1870	.1792	.1720	.1654	.1593	.1536	.1483	.1433	.1387	.1344
12	.1792	.1706	.1629	.1558	*.1493*	.1433	.1378	.1327	.1280	.1236	.1194	.1156	.1120
16	.1344	.1280	.1222	.1168	.1120	.1075	.1034	.0995	.0960	.0927	.0896	.0867	.0840
18	.1194	.1138	.1086	.1039	.0995	.0956	.0919	.0885	.0853	.0824	.0796	.0771	.0747
20	.1075	.1024	.0977	.0935	.0896	.0860	.0827	.0796	.0768	.0741	.0717	.0694	.0672
24	.0896	.0853	.0814	.0779	.0747	.0717	.0689	.0664	.0640	.0618	.0597	.0578	.0560
30	.0717	.0683	.0652	.0623	.0597	.0573	.0551	.0531	.0512	.0494	.0478	.0462	.0448
32	.0672	.0640	.0611	.0584	.0560	.0538	.0517	.0498	.0480	.0463	.0448	.0433	.0420
35	.0614	.0585	.0558	.0534	.0512	.0491	.0473	.0455	.0439	.0424	.0410	.0396	.0384
36	.0597	.0569	.0543	.0519	.0498	.0478	.0459	.0442	.0427	.0412	.0398	.0385	.0373
40	.0538	.0512	.0489	.0467	.0448	.0430	.0413	.0398	.0384	.0371	.0358	.0347	.0336
48	.0448	.0427	.0407	.0389	.0373	.0358	.0345	.0332	.0320	.0309	.0299	.0289	.0280
60	.0358	.0341	.0326	.0312	.0299	.0287	.0276	.0265	.0256	.0247	.0239	.0231	.0224
72	.0299	.0284	.0271	.0260	.0249	.0239	.0230	.0221	.0213	.0206	.0199	.0193	.0187
96	.0224	.0213	.0204	.0195	.0187	.0179	.0172	.0166	.0160	.0154	.0149	.0144	.0140
144	.0149	.0142	.0136	.0130	.0124	.0119	.0115	.0111	.0107	.0103	.0100	.0096	.0093

Example shown: *For case of 12 at 40% margin, multiply net case cost by .1493 to get retail per piece.*

10% Freight

One-Step Retail Pricing per Piece, Including Freight
for Merchandise Purchased by the Case

Markup:	50.0%	47.5%	45.0%	42.5%	40%	37.5%	35%	32.5%	30%	27.5%	25%	22.5%	20%
Case Quan: 6	.3667	.3492	.3333	.3188	.3056	.2933	.2821	.2716	.2619	.2529	.2444	.2366	.2292
10	.2200	.2095	.2000	.1913	.1833	.1760	.1692	.1630	.1571	.1517	.1467	.1419	.1375
12	.1833	.1746	.1667	.1594	*.1528*	.1467	.1410	.1358	.1310	.1264	.1222	.1183	.1146
16	.1375	.1310	.1250	.1196	.1146	.1100	.1058	.1019	.0982	.0948	.0917	.0887	.0859
18	.1222	.1164	.1111	.1063	.1019	.0978	.0940	.0905	.0873	.0843	.0815	.0789	.0764
20	.1100	.1048	.1000	.0957	.0917	.0880	.0846	.0815	.0786	.0759	.0733	.0710	.0688
24	.0917	.0873	.0833	.0797	.0764	.0733	.0705	.0679	.0655	.0632	.0611	.0591	.0573
30	.0733	.0698	.0667	.0638	.0611	.0587	.0564	.0543	.0524	.0506	.0489	.0473	.0458
32	.0688	.0655	.0625	.0598	.0573	.0550	.0529	.0509	.0491	.0474	.0458	.0444	.0430
35	.0629	.0599	.0571	.0547	.0524	.0503	.0484	.0466	.0449	.0433	.0419	.0406	.0393
36	.0611	.0582	.0556	.0531	.0509	.0489	.0470	.0453	.0437	.0421	.0407	.0394	.0382
40	.0550	.0524	.0500	.0478	.0458	.0440	.0423	.0407	.0393	.0379	.0367	.0355	.0344
48	.0458	.0437	.0417	.0399	.0382	.0367	.0353	.0340	.0327	.0316	.0306	.0296	.0286
60	.0367	.0349	.0333	.0319	.0306	.0293	.0282	.0272	.0262	.0253	.0244	.0237	.0229
72	.0306	.0291	.0278	.0266	.0255	.0244	.0235	.0226	.0218	.0211	.0204	.0197	.0191
96	.0229	.0218	.0208	.0199	.0191	.0183	.0176	.0170	.0164	.0158	.0153	.0148	.0143
144	.0153	.0146	.0139	.0133	.0127	.0122	.0118	.0113	.0109	.0105	.0102	.0099	.0095

Example shown: *For case of 12 at 40% margin, multiply net case cost by .1528 to get retail per piece.*

**12.5%
Freight**

One-Step Retail Pricing per Piece, Including Freight
for Merchandise Purchased by the Case

Markup:	50%	47.5%	45%	42.5%	40%	37.5%	35%	32.5%	30%	27.5%	25%	22.5%	20%
Case Quan: 6	.3750	.3571	.3409	.3261	.3125	.3000	.2885	.2778	.2679	.2586	.2500	.2419	.2344
10	.2250	.2143	.2045	.1957	.1875	.1800	.1731	.1667	.1607	.1552	.1500	.1452	.1406
12	.1875	.1786	.1705	.1630	*.1563*	.1500	.1442	.1389	.1339	.1293	.1250	.1210	.1172
16	.1406	.1339	.1278	.1223	.1172	.1125	.1082	.1042	.1004	.0970	.0938	.0907	.0879
18	.1250	.1190	.1136	.1087	.1042	.1000	.0962	.0926	.0893	.0862	.0833	.0806	.0781
20	.1125	.1071	.1023	.0978	.0938	.0900	.0865	.0833	.0804	.0776	.0750	.0726	.0703
24	.0938	.0893	.0852	.0815	.0781	.0750	.0721	.0694	.0670	.0647	.0625	.0605	.0586
30	.0750	.0714	.0682	.0652	.0625	.0600	.0577	.0556	.0536	.0517	.0500	.0484	.0469
32	.0703	.0670	.0639	.0611	.0586	.0563	.0541	.0521	.0502	.0485	.0469	.0454	.0439
35	.0643	.0612	.0584	.0559	.0536	.0514	.0495	.0476	.0459	.0443	.0429	.0415	.0402
36	.0625	.0595	.0568	.0543	.0521	.0500	.0481	.0463	.0446	.0431	.0417	.0403	.0391
40	.0563	.0536	.0511	.0489	.0469	.0450	.0433	.0417	.0402	.0388	.0375	.0363	.0352
48	.0469	.0446	.0426	.0408	.0391	.0375	.0361	.0347	.0335	.0323	.0313	.0302	.0293
60	.0375	.0357	.0341	.0326	.0313	.0300	.0288	.0278	.0268	.0259	.0250	.0242	.0234
72	.0313	.0298	.0284	.0272	.0260	.0250	.0240	.0231	.0223	.0216	.0208	.0202	.0195
96	.0234	.0223	.0213	.0204	.0195	.0188	.0180	.0174	.0167	.0162	.0156	.0151	.0146
144	.0156	.0149	.0142	.0136	.0130	.0125	.0120	.0116	.0112	.0108	.0104	.0101	.0098

Example shown: *For case of 12 at 40% margin, multiply net case cost by .1563 to get retail per piece.*

**15%
Freight**

One-Step Retail Pricing per Piece, Including Freight
for Merchandise Purchased by the Case

Markup:	50%	47.5%	45%	42.5%	40%	37.5%	35%	32.5%	30%	27.5%	25%	22.5%	20%
Case Quan: 6	.3833	.3651	.3485	.3333	.3194	.3067	.2949	.2840	.2738	.2644	.2556	.2473	.2396
10	.2300	.2190	.2091	.2000	.1917	.1840	.1769	.1704	.1643	.1586	.1533	.1484	.1438
12	.1917	.1825	.1742	.1667	*.1597*	.1533	.1474	.1420	.1369	.1322	.1278	.1237	.1198
16	.1438	.1369	.1307	.1250	.1198	.1150	.1106	.1065	.1027	.0991	.0958	.0927	.0898
18	.1278	.1217	.1162	.1111	.1065	.1022	.0983	.0947	.0913	.0881	.0852	.0824	.0799
20	.1150	.1095	.1045	.1000	.0958	.0920	.0885	.0852	.0821	.0793	.0767	.0742	.0719
24	.0958	.0913	.0871	.0833	.0799	.0767	.0737	.0710	.0685	.0661	.0639	.0618	.0599
30	.0767	.0730	.0697	.0667	.0639	.0613	.0590	.0568	.0548	.0529	.0511	.0495	.0479
32	.0719	.0685	.0653	.0625	.0599	.0575	.0553	.0532	.0513	.0496	.0479	.0464	.0449
35	.0657	.0626	.0597	.0571	.0548	.0526	.0505	.0487	.0469	.0453	.0438	.0424	.0411
36	.0639	.0608	.0581	.0556	.0532	.0511	.0491	.0473	.0456	.0441	.0426	.0412	.0399
40	.0575	.0548	.0523	.0500	.0479	.0460	.0442	.0426	.0411	.0397	.0383	.0371	.0359
48	.0479	.0456	.0436	.0417	.0399	.0383	.0369	.0355	.0342	.0330	.0319	.0309	.0299
60	.0383	.0365	.0348	.0333	.0319	.0307	.0295	.0284	.0274	.0264	.0256	.0247	.0240
72	.0319	.0304	.0290	.0278	.0266	.0256	.0246	.0237	.0228	.0220	.0213	.0206	.0200
96	.0240	.0228	.0218	.0208	.0200	.0192	.0184	.0177	.0171	.0165	.0160	.0155	.0150
144	.0160	.0152	.0145	.0139	.0133	.0128	.0123	.0118	.0114	.0110	.0106	.0103	.0100

Example shown: *For case of 12 at 40% margin, multiply net case cost by .1597 to get retail per piece.*

Comparisons: Weekly & Monthly, Actual vs. Target

	Sun	Mon	Tues	Wed	Thurs	Fri	Sat +		
	ec 28	29	30	31	an 1	2	3	*Week's:*	
Today	262	222	172	48	485	452	413	Total	2,053
WTD	262	483	656	703	1,188	1,640	2,053	Target	1,750
MTD					485	937	1,350		+17.4%
	4	**5**	**6**	**7**	**8**	**9**	**10**		
Today	192	196	203	193	352	400	920	Total	2,455
WTD	191	388	590	784	1,135	1,535	2,455	Target	1,750
MTD	1,542	1,738	1,941	2,134	2,486	2,886	3,806		+40.3%
	11	**12**	**13**	**14**	**15**	**16**	**17**		
Today	237	179	153	138	131	170	346	Total	1,354
WTD	237	416	569	707	838	1,008	1,354	Target	1,750
MTD	4,043	4,222	4,375	4,513	4,644	4,814	5,160		−22.6%
	18	**19**	**20**	**21**	**22**	**23**	**24**		
Today	248	185	160	141	126	184	350	Total	1,393
WTD	248	434	594	734	860	1,044	1,393	Target	1,750
MTD	5,408	5,593	5,753	5,894	6,020	6,204	6,554		−20.3%
	25	**26**	**27**	**28**	**29**	**30**	**31**		
Today	269	184	164	144	130	182	363	Total	1,435
WTD	269	453	617	761	890	1,072	1,435	Target	1,750
MTD	6,823	7,007	7,171	7,315	7,445	7,627	7,990		−17.9%

Month's Target = 7,750   +3.1%

Weekly comparisons give more frequent and more precise operational control than monthly, but the latter are useful because they match the accounts.

The amounts shown are intended only to show the set-up, and are purely arbitrary.

Index

Index